A Guide to Those Other Hummels

Hummel
Copycats
With Values

Lawrence L. Wonsch

On the cover: *Girl, HC 152/BA; Boy, HC 152/AA, Spanish
Hummel copycats. See page 102.*

Photographs: Dan Wonsch

Library of Congress Catalog
Card number 87-050012

ISBN 0-87069-497-9

Copyright© 1987
Lawrence L. Wonsch

10   9   8   7   6   5   4   3   2   1

Published by

Wallace-Homestead Book Company
580 Waters Edge
Lombard, Illinois 60148

One of the
ABC PUBLISHING
Companies

Acknowledgments

"**I** did it my way!" All by myself—in the dusty cobwebbed corner of my dimly lit attic, with haunches resting firmly on the up-end of an orange crate stuffed with yesterday's old sheet music, pen and paper on grandma's trunk, my improvised desk. With quill pen in hand, I scratched out whimsical wizzums beneath the flickering flame of a kerosene lamp, knowing its wick did not have enough light remaining to guide me through my book's final pages...." Ludicrous? Sure! But doesn't it have a nice ring to it?

Hummel Copycats is really the result of a well uncoordinated team effort. The first team is comprised of my lovely industrious wife, Millie, typing, retyping, editing, compiling tables, and writing and rewriting some sections without benefit nor pride of co-authorship. Yet she still found time to share a hug now and then. Next is my photographer son, Dan, shooting, reshooting, processing, photo-composing and editing, using whatever photographic expertise was required. Then there is Liz Fletcher, our coach, trying her utmost to organize the disorganized. Last, but surely not least, is Bill Topaz, our cheerleader, wondering if he will ever see this book in print during his lifetime. We had a lot of depth on the "bench," too, with guys and gals like Rue Dee Marker, Hank Opperman, Marc Tantillo, Robert L. and Ruth Miller, Bob Stiegler, Carol Lucas, and Dave Zuckerman. Thanks, team.

A very special mention must be made of Lucille Quine who is, relatively speaking, affectionately called Aunt Lucy. Without her, there very possibly would be no *Hummel Copycats* book. My first Dubler figurine, "Boy with Flute," was once one of her prized possessions, along with the copycat HC-1, "Puppy Love" figurine. These two were the beginning of "those other Hummels." Thank you, Aunt Lucy!

In addition to the following list, my sincere appreciation is extended to all the collectors and dealers who were most gracious in allowing us to photograph all the genuine Goebel M. I. Hummel figurines included in this book, as none belong to the author.

Patrick T. Arbenz, Sierra Vista, AZ
Florence Archambault, Newport, RI
Ted G. Arens, Milford, MI
The George Arents Research Library at
    Syracuse University, Syracuse, NY
Norman and Evelyn Blatt, Novi, MI
Hilary Cummings, Eugene, OR
Detroit Public Library, Detroit, MI
El Corte Inglés, S.A., Madrid, Spain
William J. Enright, Jr., Grosse Pointe
    Farms, MI
Mary Fante, Detroit, MI
Robert W. Gee, Torrance, CA
Dean A. Genth, Eaton, OH
Fred G. Hanna, Birmingham, MI
Vance Hanna, Birmingham, MI
Ramona Hepfner, Rochester, MI
Richard G. and Erin Hile, Grosse Pointe
    Farms, MI
John Holihan, Saint Clair Shores, MI
John F. Hotchkiss, Rochester, NY
Elizabeth Orton Jones, Mason, NH
Marie Kane, Detroit, MI
Fred and Dolores Kenneth, Babylon
    Long Island, NY

Kino International, New York, NY
Ralph and Terry Kovel, Shaker Heights, OH
Morris Kule, Elmsford, NY
Leo's Jewelry and Gifts, Wayne, MI
Carol Lucas, Bridgewater, MA
Rue Dee and Judy Marker, Sierra Vista, AZ
John Martin, Columbus, OH
Louis B. Mayer Library, American Film Institute, Los Angeles, CA
James J. and Barbara McDevitt, Fraser, MI
Mary E. McDevitt, Roseville, MI
Mildred McDevitt, Roseville, MI
Audrey Miller, Lansing, MI
Robert L. and Ruth Miller, Eaton, OH
Mother Lode Trading Co., City of East Tawas, MI
State of New York, Department of Health Bureau of Vital Records, Albany, NY
State of New York, Department of State, Division of Corporation and State Records, Albany, NY
Susan Ocana, Madrid, Spain
Occupied Japan Collector's Club, Torrance, CA
The O. J. Club, Newport, RI
Henry J. Opperman, Connellsville, PA

Tillie B. Perkins, Kakabeka Falls, Ontario, Canada
Paul and Carol Peters, Fraser, MI
Lucille W. Quine, East Detroit, MI
Ramona's Treasures, Rochester, MI
Dorothy Rebone, Detroit, MI
Roseville Public Library, Roseville, MI
Nancy Saada, Shaker Heights, OH
Al Schriber, Saint Clair Shores, MI
Gwen Shumpert, Tupelo, MS
L. E. Smith Glass Co., Mount Pleasant, PA
Bob Stiegler, Kansas City, MO
Paul J. and Gloria D. Swick, Mesa, AZ
Marc Tantillo, Elmont, NY
Uncle Winnie's, Tawas City, MI
Unicorn Gifts, Saint Clair Shores, MI
Universal City Studios Research Department, Universal City, CA
University of Oregon, The Library, Eugene, OR
George Volis, Grosse Pointe Woods, MI
Alfred E. Wick, Flushing, NY
Dee Wilkes, Mancelona, MI
Joe and Sonja Wojno, Saint Clair Shores, MI
Steven L. and Cheryl A. Wonsch, Mesa, AZ
Harvey and Kathy Wood, Mississauga, Ontario, Canada
J. C. Wyno's Antique and Collectible Shows, Saint Clair Shores, MI
David Zuckerman, Wayne, MI

Introduction

Sister Maria Innocentia Hummel was never aware that someday her wonderful art would be the genesis of a small world populated with happy, carefree orphans or Hummel gypsies, so to speak. Made from many mediums—alabaster, glass, ceramic, plaster-of-paris, plastic, porcelain, and wax—these Hummel impersonaters lurk on shelves and hide in shoeboxes, their vagabond travels taking them from my house to your house and from flea market to flea market. Who are these small boys and girls with puppy dogs and other friends, who seem so undaunted by the occasional crack or chip in their colorful armor? Where did these children come from? Who will take care of them?

Many are from established families like the Dubler kids from New York and the Beswick Hummel chaps from Beswick, England. Both of these families have Hummel connections, but many others have no true bloodline, no Hummel family and, in some instances, no proof of birthplace. They have traveled from all over the world—America, Hong Kong, Japan, Taiwan, and Spain. Despite their mixed origins, these cheerful urchins share a common bond: They are survivors and, with the exception of the Dublers, they are all Hummel copycats!

I have felt the excitement of locating these figurines in very good condition, indicating to me that a privileged few did, indeed, experience years of love and affection. Others sadden me with their display of chips and cracks, the scars of neglected years. I try to "adopt" all that I find. This book is a testament to my success in creating a happy home for "those other Hummels."

The rewards, in terms of the pleasure they've given, far outweigh the financial expenditure in accumulating these small charmers.

Unless stated otherwise in the photograph caption, the material composition of the figurine pictured is a form of that all-encompassing term, "ceramic," which includes those made of the more finely grained and harder material known as porcelain. However, all Dubler figurines are made from plaster-of-paris, unless otherwise noted. The material composition of the Spanish figurines appears to be of a harder substance—a cross between a fine grain mortar or grout material and plaster-of-paris. I have coined the name "Popware" as an interim material description until the exact material content is known.

The majority of Hummel copycats shown in the black-and-white photographs have been grouped and repeated in the Color Section and are identified by their Hummel copycat code. It was not totally possible, but we endeavored to arrange them in basic categories, such as Dublers, L. E. Smith Glass Goose Girls, Occupied Japan, musicals, and POP figurines. It would be more expedient to refer to the Index to locate that special figurine in the Color Section. Beswick figurines, except Beswick 903, are not pictured in color.

Several separate value tables are included in this book. One is a value guide to L. E. Smith Glass Goose Girls and is a part of that section. The other tables are included elsewhere and indicate the current values of all the other pieces shown, excluding Goebel's M. I. Hummel products.

Contents

How to Use This Book

A ll the Hummel copycats and Hummel-inspired pieces featured in this book, with few exceptions, are from the author's private collection. The copycat pieces are shown in black and white along with their Goebel M. I. Hummel counterpart. However, not every "Hummel-inspired" piece has an exact M. I. Hummel counterpart. Therefore, the M. I. Hummel figurine that I felt inspired its creation is compared. The only M. I. Hummel figurines pictured are those for which I have located a match or attributed an inspiration. Included in this chapter are the copycat coding prefixes, photograph description key, and label identification. I chose to use the prefix HC to identify a Hummel look-alike or copycat figurine because it seemed to be descriptive, easy to say, and easy to remember.

With each black-and-white photograph, you will find all pertinent information and comments pertaining to the item's individual peculiarities, size, markings, type of label affixed, and name, if any, assigned by the Hummel copycat maker. Each Hummel copycat has been coded with the same number that matches the production and/or mold number (excluding size indicator) incised on the bottom of its Goebel Hummel counterpart. Hummel copycat HC-1 would be the match-up to Goebel's Hum. 1 Puppy Love figurine. The figurines and other items are presented in the Goebel-Hummel numerical order in their respective sections. In two or three instances, they are numerically out of sequence, but still within a page or two of being in the proper place. For immediate detail comparison, a photograph of Goebel's M. I. Hummel counterpart is included, accompanied by the correct Hummel number, name, and trademark of that particular figurine. Other names the figurine was known by over the years appear in parentheses directly under the official Goebel name of the M. I. Hummel piece.

If you know the Hummel number of a figurine, flip through the numerical sequence pages to see if, indeed, there is a Hummel look-alike match. Unfortunately, I do not have a Hummel copycat for every Goebel Hummel produced. If you know the Hummel name of a figurine but not its number, refer to the alphabetical Index at the back of the book, which includes all the Hummels pictured in this book. If you are unable to locate the name in the Index, then there is no Hummel copycat match featured.

Value Determination

I have acquired the majority of the items shown over the past six years. Prior to 1981, I collected genuine M. I. Hummel figurines among other interesting collectibles. I take my collecting seriously and maintain a high level of perseverance, whether it be in the pursuit of Hummel copycats or Ispanky figurines. I have a propensity for detail as it applies to the proverbial "dig for information" that has long since been forgotten, fully realizing that much of yesteryear may never be remembered, let alone properly recorded by the collecting world.

The prices listed herein have been arrived at within this same dedicated framework. Most price guides tout that the prices are based on "the law of supply and demand." This certainly has validity when applied under known conditions, but it is a pricing theory that is not always applicable, particularly when one or both "supply and demand" are unknowns.

My antique and collectible appraisal experience is limited to the several areas I have collected in over the years, with my current specialty being Hummel copycats, as discussed and described herein. Unfortunately, I am unable to state, as John F. Hotchkiss did in his separate insert to *Hummel Art II, 1981 Current Price List* that reads, in part,

The basic insurance value of any example in this price list is determined by using an accumulation of over ten thousand individual postings with pertinent footnotes obtained from several hundred sources. The method used is multiple regression analysis, plotting distribution curves to determine the mean (not average) price, and the three sigma limit range.

My method of determining value for pricing purposes is more of the "kick the tire-slam the car door" approach — an unscientific, kind of down-to-earth, both feet on the ground pricing formula. Thus, the prices indicated throughout the book are of my very lonely opinion and final determination. They are being furnished as a starting point—a guideline only. Neither the author nor the publisher will be held liable for damages resulting from any loss that might be incurred when using these value tables. I have endeavored to be honest, fair, and to maintain a common-sense approach based on my personal buying and selling experience in this specialized area of collecting. I term it "fiscal rationale." The prices shown are not based on emotions or wishful thinking, nor is any item artificially inflated in price to enhance the value of my own collection for personal gain. Consequently, many of the items are priced at less than what was actually paid, and others are valued higher, based on my best judgment.

While attending a figurine auction at the 1986 International Goebel M. I. Hummel Festival in Eaton, Ohio, a Dubler, No. 48 Bawling Bennie, sold for $160. It was the only Dubler figurine being auctioned that day, and, after personally examining this piece prior to the auctioneer's opening gavel, I was prepared to bid $75 to $95 tops. It was in good to very good condition, complete with green felt-covered base and aluminum foil label. As the bidding moved rapidly past the $75 mark, I decided it would be fruitless to bid at all. It is listed in this book at $95. I paid $50 for the one in my collection.

The majority of the Hummel copycats in this book are from my personal collection, for which I negotiated the purchase of each piece. I have bought and sold duplicates, priced many others, and have exchanged pricing information with other collectors. As previously expressed, the bottom line is not always supply and demand, but it is certainly in control when the quantity of each is known.

Keep in mind there is a buyer/seller mix to be considered, which is impossible to factor into any price list, that influences each transaction. The composite mixes referred to are presented here and are not necessarily listed in the order of importance: affordability, personal priorities (degree one desires to own the item), condition, market knowledge (both buyer's and seller's), impulse buying, and type of sale (auction, antique show, dealer, flea market, garage sale). Other factors: Does the seller have a cash flow problem, forcing his price down? Is the buyer "flush"? Or maybe the collector is "possessed" with his hobby (must have at any cost). The list goes on and on. Any or all of these unrecorded influences do not determine a true sustained current value—only a price paid or received at a particular point in time.

The values listed are not "etched in stone." They are a guide. The prices are based on POP (plaster-of-paris) pieces being in *very good condition* with only one or two minute paint chips being acceptable. The Dubler figurines *must have* green felt-covered bases with the appropriate aluminum foil label affixed. *All other prices apply to mint condition pieces,* even though not all of the photographed examples in the book match this standard of quality. You may elect to add a certain percentage to values shown when selling or discount them when making an offer or use as shown. Only you can decide their worth. Hopefully, this book will aid you in your decision.

My closing recommendation: Buy yourself a Japanese abacus (MIOJ preferred), tuck a copy of *Hummel Copycats* under your arm, and head out into the collectibles jungle. Hang the cost—you'll love the hunt.

Key to Symbols

Hummel Copycat code: HC—Hummel copycat; HCM—mini-size; BE—bookend; BVS—bud vase; CDL—candleholder; MBX—music box; MC—Mel copycat; PLQ—plaque; PLQF—plaque figurine; PTR—planter; REL—religious message figurine; RMF—revolving musical figurine; SPS—salt and pepper shakers; TLP—table lamp; TPK—toothpick holder; WVS—wall vase. *Note:* Unless otherwise specified, all copycats pictured are made of ceramic.

9

Copycat Labels and Marks

D1—foil label, black on gold, 1⁵⁄₁₆″ diameter.

D2—foil label, black on gold, 1¼″ diameter.

D3—paper label, white on blue, 1¼″ diameter.

D4—foil label, blue on gold, ⅞″ h × 1⁵⁄₁₆″ w.

D5—foil label, black on gold, 1³⁄₁₆″ diameter.

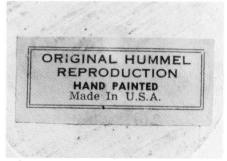

D6—paper label, dark blue on white, ¾″ h × 1¹¹⁄₁₆″ w.

D7—foil label, green on gold, ½ ″ h × 1¼ ″ w.

D8—paper label, green on white, ½ ″ h × 1¼ ″ w.

D9—foil label, black on gold, 1″ h × 1½ ″ w.

D10—foil label, black on gold, ¾ ″ h × ½ ″ w.

D11—no label, marked black ink, 1¼ ″ h × 1⁵⁄₁₆″ w.

D12—foil label, red on gold, 1½ ″ diameter, c. 1965. Found affixed to the frame holding a Hummel postcard produced by Verlag Emil Fink, Stuttgart, Germany. Note the interesting logo style of the Das Hummele (bumblebee).

Sister Maria Innocentia Hummel (Berta Hummel, Artist)

The life of Sister Maria Innocentia Hummel has been detailed extensively in the many collectors' books published over the years. The devout Hummel collector knows her background well. But for the layman and collector of "those other Hummels," this synopsis will provide an informative prelude.

Sister Maria Innocentia, born Berta Hummel on May 21, 1909, in the village of Massing in southern Bavaria, revealed her sense of humor and vivid imagination at an early age. Prior to entering school at age six, she was acting out German fairy tales and folklore for her family and friends, adding her own precocious touch. But her drawings were the medium that best displayed her impetuous wit. While her father, a successful merchant as a civilian, was serving in the German Army in World War I, she cheered him with her postcards and notes that were edged with clever sketches of amusing incidents. Berta's father, having an inherent aptitude for and love of art, recognized this artistic ability even then and encouraged her to further her creative education.

After attending Catholic schools, Berta entered the Academy of Fine and Applied Arts in Munich in 1927, where she was influenced artistically by Professor Max Dasio, who considered her his protege. While in attendance there she became close friends with two nuns who ultimately were influential in her decision to enter the Franciscan Convent of Siessen in 1931. When she took her final vows in 1933, she selected Maria Innocentia as her religious name.

Sister Maria Innocentia maintained a sense of humor throughout the convent years. Daily contact with the children she loved inspired her sketches and drawings that so aptly portrayed the appealing innocence of childhood.

The Sister's artwork, in the form of prints and postcards, was first published in 1933 by Joseph Müller, Verlag Ars Sacra in Munich. In 1934, Franz Goebel of the W. Goebel firm of Rödental, Germany, approached Sister Maria Innocentia and the Siessen Convent seeking a license to transfer her two-dimensional drawings into three-dimensional form. They eventually entered into an agreement that provided Sister Hummel, and later the Siessen Convent, with final approval authority of all figurine adaptations prior to their initial production and distribution. In return, the convent was to receive recompense in the form of royalties. It is reported that the convent has been paid millions of dollars over the years due to this royalty agreement, and the ensuing success of this business venture for the W. Goebel firm is now legendary.

The first figurines bearing the now famous M. I. Hummel facsimile signature were introduced at the 1935 Leipzig Trade Fair. This trademark, then and now, indicates that the figurines are genuine adaptations of Sister Hummel's artwork after she entered the Siessen Convent.

Ill for several years, Sister Maria Innocentia Hummel died of tuberculosis on November 6, 1946, at Siessen. Fortunately, the mischievous, yet innocent faces of her *kinder* live on today through her many drawings and sketches—the genesis of the beloved Hummel figurines.

In this book you will find many of "those other Hummels" possessing a similar but quizzical facial expression, which surely wonders, "M. I. Hummel or am I not?"

Hummel Collectors' Clubs

Recommended clubs: Two principal clubs I can recommend from personal experience because I am a member of both organizations are:

Goebel Collectors' Club
Division of Goebel Art GmbH
105 White Plains Road
Tarrytown, New York 10591
Club vice-president and editor:
Joan N. Ostroff
Publication: Quarterly newsletter titled *Insights*
Annual membership dues: $20.

"Hummel" Collectors' Club, Inc.
1261 University Drive
P.O. Box 257
Yardley, Pennsylvania 19067
Club president and editor:
Dorothy Dous
Publication: Quarterly Newsletter
Annual Membership Dues: $20.

Numerical Photographic Section

Figurines, Candleholders, and Bookends

Goebel's genuine M. I. Hummel figurines are often referred to as reproductions of Sister Hummel's works of art. In reality, these transformations of her two-dimensional art into three-dimensional figurines could be termed adaptations. Authentic M. I. Hummel figurines might actually be looked upon as reproductions of themselves.

Over the years the many terms "Hummel look-alike," "Hummel reproduction," "Hummel copy," "pseudo Hummel," "fake Hummel," have come to epitomize any-thing produced to look like the genuine (approved by the Siessen Convent) Goebel Hummel figurines incised with the autho-rized "M. I. Hummel" facsimile signature. This is not only the popular consensus, but is the widely accepted meaning.

This book introduces, with current values, the wide variety of copycats and inspirations produced over the years in their many forms, from figurines to wall vases. You be the judge—M. I. Hummel or am I not?

Photograph key: MIOJ—Made in Occupied Japan; POP—plaster-of-paris; OJ—Occupied Japan; USA—United States of America; (b)—black ink mark; (g)—green ink mark; (r)—red ink mark.

A question mark (?) following the origin indicates an unmarked piece and the author's best guess as to its origin. NQV appearing in various tables throughout the book indicates there is no quoted value for that particular item.

Hummel copycat label identification: See label photographs on page 10.

Puppy Love, Hum. 1
("Little Violinist," "Little Fiddler with Dog")

One of ten figurines introduced in 1935 at the Leipzig Trade Fair in Germany. Made by Goebel always wearing a black hat. Old style Goebel Hum. 1, without bow tie and with a slightly different head angle is considered rare. See PTR's 1A, 1B, 1C, 1D, and 1E, Planter section, for five Hummel-inspired Puppy Love planters.

Hum. 1 Puppy Love, TMK-6.

HC-1A, USA, POP, D1 label, 5″.

HC-1B, MIOJ(b), 4¾″, blue hat.

HC-1C, Japan, 5⅜″. Umbrella handle missing.

HC-1D, MIOJ(r), 4¼″.

HC-1E, MIOJ(g), 5⅛″. I have one other identical edition of this figurine marked "Japan" only.

14

Little Fiddler, Hum. 2 & 4
("Violinist," "The Wandering Fiddler," "Little Fiddler without Dog")

Goebel Hum. 2 was restyled in 1972, with brown hat. Otherwise same as Goebel Hum. 4 and Puppy Love, Hum. 1, minus dog. Goebel Hum. 4, same as Goebel Hum. 2, except has black hat. See SPS-2A, Salt and Pepper Shaker section, for one Hummel-inspired Little Fiddler salt shaker.

Hum. 2/0 Little Fiddler, TMK-6.

HC-2A, MIOJ(b), 4⅜", green hat.

HC-2B, MIOJ(r), 4⅞", no umbrella.

HC-2C, MIOJ(r), 4½", yellow hat, no umbrella.

HC-2D, USA, POP, D9 label, 7¾".

HC-4A, USA(?), POP, no label, 5", black hat.

HC-4B, Unknown origin, 5", no umbrella, black hat.

15

Strolling Along, Hum. 5
("Wanderer with Dog")

This is another figurine that made its debut at the 1935 Leipzig Trade Fair. Early models featured eyes that glanced to the side similar to HC-5C. The restyled version shows him looking straight out as seen in Goebel Hum. 5, Strolling Along. See Beswick Hummel figurine No. 906, Strolling Along, in the Beswick Hummel section.

Hum. 5 Strolling Along, restyled version, TMK-6.

HC-5A, USA(?), POP, no label, 5⅞".

REL-5A, USA(?), POP, no label, 4⅞". Incised edge of base "© 1947." Sign reads, "Jesus Said, 'I Am The Way.'"

HC-5B, Taiwan, 6⅝". Very good color and detail. See companion figurines HC-7E, HC-79E, and Color Section.

HC-5C, OJ(b), 5". Umbrella handle and dog's tail missing.

Key to Symbols

Hummel Copycat code: HC—Hummel copycat; HCM—mini-size; BE—bookend; BVS—bud vase; CDL—candle-holder; MBX—music box; MC—Mel copycat; PLQ—plaque; PLQF—plaque figurine; PTR—planter; REL—religious message figurine; RMF—revolving musical figurine; SPS—salt and pepper shakers; TLP—table lamp; TPK—toothpick holder; WVS—wall vase. *Note:* Unless otherwise specified, all copycats pictured are made of ceramic.

Merry Wanderer, Hum. 7 & 11

Produced since 1935 in several sizes and number of button variations. Goebel Hum. 11, 4¼ " size, sometimes found with a six- or seven-button vest in place of five-button style normally provided on Goebel Hum. 7 and Hum. 11. Older Goebel models were mounted on a simple double base that is not as exaggerated in appearance as the bases of HC-7B and HC-7C. See RMF-7A, Revolving Musical Figurines section, for one Hummel inspired Merry Wanderer revolving musical figurine. Merry Wanderer is the most visible figurine in the Goebel line. This model is used extensively in their promotional advertising to the extent that larger-than-life-size figures adorn the grounds outside the Goebel plant in Rödental, West Germany, and the Goebel Collectors' Club in Tarrytown, New York.

Hum. 7/0 Merry Wanderer, TMK-3.

HC-7A, Hong Kong, wax, D10 label, 5¾ ".

HC-7B, USA, POP, D7 label reads "Coventry Ware," 5½ ", double base, cork-covered.

HC-7C, Unknown origin, 5 ", double base.

HC-7D, Japan, 4⅝". Note position of umbrella.

HC-7E, Taiwan, 6⅞". Very good color and detail (except has oval base). See HC-5B, HC-79E and Color Section.

17

Book Worm, Hum. 8

("Little Book Worm")

Also see Beswick No. 904, Book Worm, in the Beswick Hummel section.

Hum. 8 Book Worm, book pictures in color, TMK-6.

HC-8A, USA, POP, D7 label reads "Coventry Ware," 4", cork-covered base.

Flower Madonna, Hum. 10
("Virgin with Flowers," "Sitting Madonna with Child")

Although made of plaster-of-paris type material HC-10A is a close replica of Goebel's older edition of Hum. 10, Flower Madonna, with the open doughnut style halo. It is complete with an incised "M. I. Hummel" signature on the back lower base. Hummel experts were unable to provide documentation of its origin, although some perceive the possibility that it was of Herbert Dubler manufacture. I am not convinced this is a Dubler figurine. It appears that a mold made from a Goebel Flower Madonna was used to produce this plaster-of-paris replica. This unique piece resides in the Rue Dee Marker collection. See HC-23B, Adoration, HC-28A, Wayside Devotion, and HC-59A, Skier, for similarly produced and signed POP replicas. Also see Color Section.

Hum. 10/I Flower Madonna with open halo, TMK-2.

HC-10A, USA(?), POP, no label, 8⅝". Cream/ivory. Incised with "M. I. Hummel" signature.

HC-10A (back view).

19

Meditation, Hum. 13
("The Little Messenger," "The Well Wisher")

Meditation, Hum. 13, was originally made by Goebel with a partially filled basket of flowers. Restyling in early 1960s resulted in removal of the flowers. The large Goebel Hum. 13/V, 13¾″ high, features a full basket of flowers. Several known sizes and basket variations were produced by Goebel over the years. See PTR-13A, Planter section, for one Hummel-inspired Meditation planter. Also see Beswick figurine No. 910, Meditation, in the Beswick Hummel section.

Hum. 13/0 Meditation, no flowers, TMK-3.

HC-13A, Japan, 5″.

HC-13B, OJ(b), "American Children, I Bring Greetings"(r), 5¼″, round base.

HC-13C, Japan(?), 5″. Full basket of flowers, round base.

HC-13D, USA(?), POP, no label, 5⅜″.

Key to Symbols

Hummel Copycat code: HC—Hummel copycat; HCM—mini-size; BE—bookend; BVS—bud vase; CDL—candleholder; MBX—music box; MC—Mel copycat; PLQ—plaque; PLQF—plaque figurine; PTR—planter; REL—religious message figurine; RMF—revolving musical figurine; SPS—salt and pepper shakers; TLP—table lamp; TPK—toothpick holder; WVS—wall vase. *Note:* Unless otherwise specified, all copycats pictured are made of ceramic.

Book Worm, Bookends, Hum. 14/A & B

The books held by boy bookends BE-14/AA, BE-14/AB, and BE-14/AD, have the same two pictures as the book held by their Goebel Hum. 14/A counterpart. Right-hand page shows a house with smoke billowing from its chimney; opposite page has a large snail. The pair of POP Bookends, BE-14/BA and BE-14/AA, are too small to actually be used as bookends. The four ceramic pieces shown appear to be from four different manufacturers and are weighted by filling with sand, then corked with a stopper. See PTR-14/BA, Planter section, for one Hummel-inspired girl Book Worm bookend.

Hum. 14/B Book Worm, girl, Bookend, TMK-3. Robert L. Miller collection.

Hum. 14/A Book Worm, boy, Bookend, TMK-2. Robert L. Miller collection.

BE-14/BA, USA, POP, D7 label reads "Coventry Ware," 4", cork-lined base.

BE-14/AA, USA, POP, reads "Coventry Ware," D7 label, 4", cork-lined base.

BE-14/BB, MIOJ(r), 5⅝".

BE-14/AB, MIOJ(b), 5½".

BE-14/AC, Japan(?), 6".

BE-14AD, Japan, 5¼".

Hum. 15/0 Hear Ye, Hear
Ye, TMK-5.

Hear Ye, Hear Ye, Hum. 15
("Night Watchman")

Although HC-15B and HC-15C show the Hummel copycats
mounted on a double base, Goebel never produced a Hear Ye,
Hear Ye, Hum. 15, on such a base. Color variations of mittens
do exist on both Goebel models and their HC parallels. See
RMF-15A, Revolving Musical Figurines section, for Hummel-
inspired Hear Ye, Hear Ye revolving musical figurine.

HC-15A, USA, POP, D4
label, 5⅜".

HC-15B, USA(?), POP, no
label, 5⅝". Double base.

HC-15C, USA, POP, D7
label, "Coventry Ware,"
5⅝". Double base, cork
covered.

HC-15D, Japan(?), 4⅜". No
mittens.

HC-15E, Japan, 5⅜". With
pennant instead of blade on
staff, no mittens, oval base.

Little Hiker, Hum. 16
("Happy-Go-Lucky," "Hans in Fortune")

Goebel's Hum. 16, Little Hiker, has managed to escape major design changes since introduction in 1935. Produced over the years by Goebel in several sizes ranging from 4″ to 6″.

Many Little Hiker copycats have also been produced, as attested to by the numerous variations shown herein. These examples range in size from 4″ to 5½″, with the BE-16A bookend measuring 6″ high.

Dogs, large and small, were popular additions to some of the look-alikes, even though no dogs were included with the Goebel figure. The producers may have thought that by adding a dog, duck, songbird, or rocking horse, no one would notice they had faithfully copied the genuine M. I. Hummel figurine. See SPS-16A, Salt and Pepper Shaker section, for one Hummel-inspired Little Hiker shaker.

Hum. 16/2/0 Little Hiker, TMK-5.

(L) HC-16B, Japan, 4″. (R) HC-16C, Japan, 4¼″. Both are free-standing.

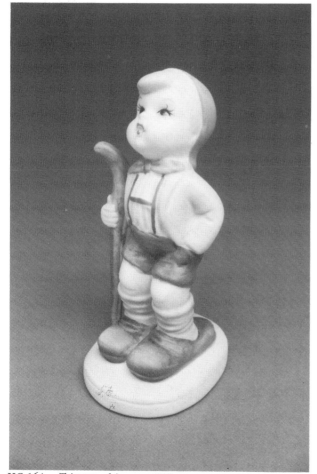

HC-16A, Taiwan, bisque, 5¼″.

HC-16D, USA, POP, D7 label, "Coventry Ware," cork-covered base, 5⅛″.

23

Little Hiker (continued)

HC-16E, Unknown origin, 5".

HC-16F, USA(?), POP, no label, 5½".

BE-16A, Japan, 6" h × 5" w × 3½" d, Bookend.

HC-16G, Japan(?), with white overglaze, 5⅛".

HC-16H, MIOJ(r), 5⅜".

Hummel Corner

Since October, 1938, nothing stamped "Hummel" has come out of the little convent in Siessen, Bavaria, where the gentle nun, Sister Berta Hummel, for years created the lovable figures which have endeared themselves to millions the world over. Here, however, are enchanting pieces capturing all the color and charm of Sister Hummel's originals, from which they were made, and expressing her artistry and her love for little children.

Goose Children—2012. Famous Goose Boy and Goose Girl figurines, superbly hand colored. They are about 5¼" tall and perfectly formed in fine ceramic. Each one carries a stamp marking it as a genuine Hummel reproduction. Refreshing for display in the nursery, or wherever a lovely figure can help a nook to greater charm. State style. Each, **$1.40.**

Framed Picture — 2002. Winsome prints of Hummel children, of which the above is typical. Print framed in ivory matting, under glass. 7½" x 9½" overall. Natural-finish light wood frame of half-inch wood. Each, **$1.15.**

Book Ends—2013. The famous wistful Rabbit Boy in a pair of book ends perfect for any child's room! Each piece is of fine and heavy ceramic, carefully molded and artfully hand colored. Bottoms are felted, of course, to protect furniture surfaces. Ample bases to take any number of books Junior has. Pair, **$2.95.**

Informal Cards—2001. A collectors' box of 20 cards, each 3¼" x 4" folded, and each featuring a full color reproduction of a Hummel child on its cover. Cards present three pages for writing messages—thank you's, invitations, greetings, etc., and the box is complete with envelopes. Cards are printed in soft tones of rich colors on fancy-finish white card stock. Per box of 20, **$1.**

Featured on page 63 of *Miles Kimball of Oshkosh* catalog, Fall and Winter 1946-47 edition. Courtesy of Carol Lucas.

25

Congratulations, Hum. 17
("I Congratulate")

Old style, no socks. Socks added early 1970s. See RMF-17A, Revolving Musical Figurines section, for one Hummel-inspired Congratulations revolving musical figurine.

Hum. 17/0 Congratulations, no socks, TMK-3.

HC-17A, USA(?), POP, no label, 5 ¾ ", no socks.

Prayer Before Battle, Hum. 20
("The Pious Horseman")

HC-20B, Little Knight, is from the American Children series. The quality of American Children figurines is far superior to that of most other HC figurines. However, they still fall short quality-wise, when compared to the genuine Goebel M. I. Hummels and the English Hummels produced by Beswick. Refer to the Occupied Japan section for further discussion. See PTR-20A, Planter section, for one Hummel-inspired Prayer Before Battle planter.

Hum. 20 Prayer Before Battle, TMK-2.

HC-20A, USA(?), POP, no label, 4¼".

HC-20B, OJ(b), "American Children, Little Knight"(r), 4¾".

27

Heavenly Angel, Hum. 21
("Celestial Messenger," "Little Guardian")

Hum. 21/0/½ Heavenly
Angel, TMK-1.

HC-21A, USA(?), POP, no label, 4 ¼ ".

Adoration, Hum. 23
("Ave Maria," "At the Shrine," "At Mother Maria's")

Both HC-23A and HC-23B are exceptionally good Hummel copycats. The large HC-23B shown has the "M. I. Hummel" facsimile signature incised on back edge of base. See HC-10A Flower Madonna, HC-28A Wayside Devotion, and HC-59A Skier for similarly produced and signed POP replicas.

Hum. 23/1 Adoration, TMK-2.

HC-23A, Japan, 6½". Silver on blue foil label reads "Ajax, Made in Japan."

HC-23B, USA(?), POP, no label, 8¾". "M. I. Hummel" incised signature. Robert L. Miller collection.

Angelic Sleep, Candleholder, Hum. 25
("Angel's Joy")

Angelic Sleep, Candleholder, Hum. 25, was produced by Goebel in color and in a rare white overglaze. It was only made in the 3½" × 5" size. Interestingly, I have two Hummel copycats in my collection, HC-25A and HC-25B, one slightly smaller and the other considerably larger than Goebel's Hum. 25. The major difference is that my two were made without candle sockets. Nevertheless, they are excellent look-alikes.

Hum. 25 Angelic Sleep, Candleholder, TMK-3. Robert L. Miller collection.

HC-25A, MIOJ(g), 3⅛" h × 4¼" w. Made without candleholder.

HC-25B, MIOJ(g), 4⅛" h × 5⅞" w. Made without candleholder.

Wayside Devotion, Hum. 28
("Evening Song," "The Little Shepherd")

Introduced in 1935 by Goebel, Wayside Devotion, Hum. 28, at one time was produced in a white overglaze, now considered rare. During the 1970s, Goebel introduced a similar figurine, except without shrine, named Eventide, Hum. 99. The intriguing feature of this Hummel copycat is the M. I. Hummel "signature" incised center back of base. I know of only three other POP figurines signed like this: Flower Madonna, HC-10A, Adoration, HC-23B, and Skier, HC-59A. The origin of these four figurines is still unknown to me and must be left, for the moment, to conjecture.

Hum. 28/2 Wayside Devotion, TMK-2.

HC-28A, USA(?), POP, no label, 7 ¼ ". M. I. Hummel incised "signature."

HC-28A (back view).

31

Angel, Joyous News with Lute, Hum. 38
("The Little Advent Angel with Lute")

Angel, Joyous News with Accordion, Hum. 39

Angel, Joyous News with Trumpet, Hum. 40

Hum. I/38/0 Angel, Joyous News with Lute, Candleholder, TMK-2.

As a three-piece set, called "Angel Trio (B)" candleholders by Goebel. See Angel Trio (B) Set, Hum. 238/A, B, C. Unlike their "free-sitting" Goebel Hummel counterparts, the Hummel copycats CDL-38A, CDL-39A, CDL-40A are each mounted with their candleholder on an oval base. Note the correct positions of the copycats' wings.

Hum. I/39/0 Angel, Joyous News with Accordion, Candleholder, TMK-2.

Hum. I/40/0 Angel, Joyous News with Trumpet, Candleholder, TMK-2.

CDL-38A, MIOJ(r), 2⅞".

CDL-39A, MIOJ(r), 2 ¾ ".

CDL-40A, MIOJ(r), 2⅞".

33

Good Shepherd, Hum. 42

Hum. 42/0 Good Shepherd, TMK-2.

HC-42A, USA(?), POP, no label, 6⅛″.

March Winds, Hum. 43
("Rascal," "Urchin")

March Winds, Goebel's Hum. 43, is found in many size variations and, according to John F. Hotchkiss in his book *Hummel Art II*, "when issued, it carried the German name *Lausbub* for 'Rascal,' the name given to it by Sister Hummel."

Hum. 43 March Winds, TMK-6.

HC-43A, USA(?), POP, no label, 4⅞".

HC-43B, Japan, 4¾".

35

Hum. 47/0 Goose Girl, TMK-5.

Goose Girl, Hum. 47
("Little Gooseherd")

Two views of HC-47A, a very desirable Hummel copycat, show the "blade of grass" sprouting between geese. This feature, found only on some earlier Goebel Hum. 47, Goose Girl models, warrants a premium price. Consequently, the value is also greater when discovered on an HC figurine. Value of this example is further enhanced by its being marked "Made in Occupied Japan." Goebel's Goose Girl, Hum. 47, a very popular Hummel figurine, was widely imitated and produced by others, as attested to by the many examples shown herein. She can be found in porcelain, plastic, plaster-of-paris, and even glass. See section on L. E. Smith glass Goose Girls. Also see PTR-47A, PTR-47B, and BVS-47A in Planter section for two

(L) HC-47A, MIOJ(g), 5¼". **(R)** HCM-47A, Japan(?), 3", mini-sized.

HC-47A (side view), with blade of grass between geese.

HC-47B, Hong Kong, plastic, 3⅞".

HC-47C, MIOJ(r), 4½".

HC-47D, USA, POP, D2 label, 4¾".

HC-47E, Japan, 5".

36

Hummel-inspired Goose Girl planters and one bud vase. See RMF-47A, Revolving Musical Figurines section, for one Hummel-inspired revolving musical figurine, and Beswick No. 905, Goose Girl, in the Beswick Hummel section.

HC-47F, USA(?), POP, no label, 5⅜".

HC-47G, Japan, with white overglaze, 5".

HC-47H, Japan(?), 5⅝".

HC-47J, USA(?), POP, no label, 7⅜".

Goose Girl Table Lamp, TLP-47A

Although unmarked as to origin, my best guess is USA. This piece has no Hummel counterpart lamp. The figurine itself is a nice rendering of Goebel's Hum. 47, Goose Girl and exemplifies surprisingly good detail and color, as do many of the plaster-of-paris-type Hummel copycats. I have not seen another like it.

TLP-47A, USA(?), POP, no label, 7¾" h × 5" w. Standard 120v socket inside basket.

TLP-47A (side view).

To Market, Hum. 49
("Brother and Sister")

To Market, Hum. 49, was modeled in 1936. Note 4″ high size is always without bottle in basket. According to *Hotchkiss' Handbook to Hummel Art,* "No original drawing or graphic in this exact design has been located." The boy looks like Trumpet Boy, Hum. 97, except without horn. Or possibly Brother, Hum. 95, without his hat, was joined on a common base with Sister, Hum. 98, to create Goebel's Hum. 49, To Market. See HC-97/98A for Hummel copycat Trumpet Boy and Sister mounted on a common oval base.

Hum. 49/3/0 To Market, TMK-5.

HC-49A, Japan, 4¾″, bottle in basket.

HC-49B, MIOJ(b), 4½″, flowers in basket.

HC-49C, Japan, 5⅛″, bottle in basket.

HC-49D, MIOJ(r), 5⅜″, bottle in basket.

HC-49E, Japan(?), 5⅛″, bottle standing erect inside front of basket.

HC-49F, USA, POP, D8 label reads "Coventry Ware," 5⅜″, no bottle, cork-lined base.

39

Volunteers, Hum. 50
("Playing Soldiers")

Volunteers, Hum. 50, was produced by Goebel in sizes from 5″ to 6½″ high. The Hummel copycats shown are well within this size range. Note the oval base on both HC-50A and HC-50B, even though Goebel's Hum. 50, Volunteers, was made only with a square base.

Hum. 50/I Volunteers, TMK-6.

HC-50A, Japan, 5⅛″, oval base, dog added.

HC-50B, MIOJ(g), 5¼″, oval base, dog added.

HC-50C, Japan, 6¼″, square base.

HC-50D, Japan(?), 5⅝″, square base, dog added.

Reproduction of Sister Hummel drawing on 5½″ × 4″ folded notecard No. 10 H 313 printed, published, and copyrighted in the U.S. in 1943 by Ars Sacra, Herbert Dubler, Inc., New York.

Village Boy, Hum. 51
("Country Boy")

See TPK-51A, Planter section, for one Hummel-inspired Village Boy toothpick holder.

Hum. 51/0 Village Boy, TMK-3.

HC-51A, Hong Kong, plastic, 4½″, round base.

Going to Grandma's, Hum. 52

("Housemothers")

Two views of HC-52A, a highly unique Hummel copycat, are shown here. It is an exceptionally good copy of Goebel's old-style rectangular base Going to Grandma's, Hum. 52. Like its smaller Hummel counterpart pictured, this copycat is carrying candy inside its cone; whereas, the cone held by the girl in the larger Goebel figurine (not shown) is empty.

HC-52A has a cork stopper in the back of one figure and contained a syrup-type liquid when I bought it at an antique show in Livonia, Michigan. This piece has aged gracefully, and I would date it early 1940s. Any information concerning the manufacture and/or distribution of this particular figurine would be most welcome. I would appreciate hearing from those who have knowledge of a similar Hummel copycat produced as a vessel for holding liquid or other substance.

Hum. 52/0 Going to Grandma's, TMK-3.

HC-52A, Unknown origin, 4⅜". Unique.

HC-52A back view shows cork stopper.

Joyful, Hum. 53
("Banjo Betty," "Singing Lesson," "Singing Rehearsal")

Hum. 53 Joyful, TMK-6.
Wears an orange dress in
some older examples.

HC-53A, USA(?), POP, no
label, 3¼". Brown dress.

HC-53C, MIOJ(b), 3⅞". Green dress.

HC-53B, Japan, 4⅛",
marked "Gold Castle."
Orange dress.

Silent Night, Candleholder, Hum. 54

Hum. 54 Silent Night, Candleholder, TMK-2.

According to *Hotchkiss' Handbook to Hummel Art,* page 32, "This model can be and frequently is confused with Hum. 31. The Hum. 31 black child wears an earring but no shoes; the hair is smooth and less detailed than that of the same white children in Hum. 54." Also this figurine is sometimes mistaken for Hum. 113 Heavenly Song, Candleholder. To add to the confusion, Goebel's Hum. 54 figurine on page 32 of the *Handbook* is shown in reverse profile, and since this book is a condensed version of *Hummel Art II,* that photograph is also incorrect. The color separations used in the printing of these two photographs were erroneously inverted. I feel this should be brought to the reader's attention, since the *Handbook* is such a handy reference for the collector. Particularly in the event one does have a CDL-54 Hummel copycat they are trying to identify.

CDL-54A, Japan(?), 4″ h × 5½″ w × 3¼″ d, excellent color, detail, and size. This copy includes an integral 2″ red porcelain candle.

Out of Danger, Hum. 56/B
("Girl in Safety")

New model has eyes of girl looking down. In older edition her eyes are wide open.

Hum. 56/B Out of Danger, TMK-6.

HC-56/BA, Taiwan, bisque, 6¾", looking down.

Culprits, Hum. 56/A
("Apple Thief, Boy")

Hum. 56/A Culprits, TMK-6.

Culprits, Hum. 56, was originally made in 1935 without branch at boy's foot and with boy's eyes wide open, similar to HC 56/AA. Later redesigned with the addition of a branch at the boy's foot and boy looking down at dog as per Goebel's Culprits, Hum. 56/A and HC 56/AB. As a collector, I find it exciting to locate both the old and new copycat versions, which I am quite certain were inspired by Goebel's M. I. Hummel counterparts.

Note: Culprits look-alike figurine HC-56/AB and the companion Out of Danger HC-56/BA on the preceding page were offered for sale by Cook Bros., Inc., Chicago, Illinois, in their *Wholesale Catalog 1985-86.* This pair is featured on the catalog cover and on page 30. Both are listed as "#53024 Hummel Style Kids in Tree. . .A, B 7″ H $15.90 Ea." A nice item even at the $15.90 each suggested list price.

HC-56/AA, USA, POP, D2 label, 6¼″, eyes open, no foot branch.

HC-56/AB, Taiwan, bisque, 6⅝″, looking down. Has foot branch, but is minus fallen apple.

Chick Girl, Hum. 57
("Little Chick Mother," "The Little Chick Girl")

Goebel's Hum. 57, Chick Girl, is found in several sizes. The small size has two, and the larger size has three chicks in her basket. See Hummel look-alike BE-61/BA in Bookend section, and Hummel-inspired MBX-57A in Music Box section.

Hum. 57/0 Chick Girl, TMK-5.

HC-57A, Japan, Napco label, 4″, two-chick basket. Marked "Chickadee AH1D." Harvey and Kathy Wood Collection.

HC-57B, USA(?), POP, no label, 4⅜″, three-chick basket.

HC-57C, USA, POP, 4⅜″, three-chick basket. Marked "#614 made by Lucille Morrison Princeton Kentucky." (D11 mark.)

HC-57D, Unknown origin, 3¾″, two-chick basket.

HC-57E, MIOJ(b), 4″, two-chick basket.

47

Playmates, Hum. 58
("Just Friends," "Rabbit Father")

Compare all the Hummel copycats on this page and note the subtle differences between each. All are very similar, yet not alike; slight variations can be seen in facial expressions, head positions, eyes, and thickness and diameter of bases. Figurine HC-58B was made without bow tie. HC-58C has all the rabbits' ears down. Compare the fine detail of HC-58A to Goebel's Playmates, Hum. 58. Also see BE-61/AA in Bookend section and Hummel-inspired MBX-58A in Music Box section.

Hum. 58/0 Playmates, TMK-6.

HC-58A, Japan, 4⅛", marked "PALS SH3C." Doughnut-style base.

HC-58B, USA(?), POP, no label, 4⅜". Feather in hat not prominent, no bow tie.

HC-58C, USA, POP, D1 label, 4½", rabbits' ears down.

HC-58D, USA, POP, D2 label, 4⅜".

Key to Symbols

Hummel Copycat code: HC—Hummel copycat; HCM—mini-size; BE—bookend; BVS—bud vase; CDL—candleholder; MBX—music box; MC—Mel copycat; PLQ—plaque; PLQF—plaque figurine; PTR—planter; REL—religious message figurine; RMF—revolving musical figurine; SPS—salt and pepper shakers; TLP—table lamp; TPK—toothpick holder; WVS—wall vase. *Note:* Unless otherwise specified, all copycats pictured are made of ceramic.

Skier, Hum. 59
("Hail, Skiing")

The plaster-of-paris figurine, HC-59A, appears to be another exact replica of a Goebel Hummel figure. This time it is of Goebel's Hum. 59, Skier. Like the HC-10A, Flower Madonna, HC-23B, Adoration, and HC-28A, Wayside Devotion replicas, it also bears an M. I. Hummel incised signature. Comments and conclusions with regard to those copycats also apply to this figure.

Hum. 59 Skier, TMK-5

HC-59A, USA(?), POP, no label, 5¼", very good color, detail and size. Incised "signature."

HC-59A (back view).

Farm Boy, Bookend, Hum. 60/A

Hum. 60/A Farm Boy,
Bookend, TMK-2. Robert
L. Miller collection.

BE-60/AA, Spain, Popware figurine is 4½".

Goose Girl, Bookend, Hum. 60/B

Both wooden bookends are 5¾" h × 4⅝" w ×4⅞" d, with
red felt covered bases. See section on Spanish Hummels for
detailed discussion.

Hum. 60/B Goose Girl,
Bookend, TMK-2. Robert
L. Miller collection.

BE-60/BA, Spain, Popware figurine is 4¼".

Playmates, Bookend, Hum. 61/A

Hum. 61/A Playmates, Bookend, TMK-2. Robert L. Miller collection.

BE-61/AA, Spain, Popware figurine is 4⅝″.

Chick Girl, Bookend, Hum. 61/B

Both wooden bookends are 5¾″h × 4½″w × 4¾″d, with red felt covered bases. See section on Spanish Hummels for detailed discussion.

Hum. 61/B Chick Girl, Bookend, TMK-2. Robert L. Miller collection.

BE-61/BA, Spain, Popware figurine is 4⅜″.

Singing Lesson, Hum 63
("Duet," "Critic")

See PTR-63A, PTR-63B, and WVS-63A, Planter section, for two Hummel-inspired Singing Lesson planters and one wall vase.

Hum. 63 Singing Lesson, TMK-6.

HC-63C, USA(?), POP, no label, 2¾".

HC-63B, MIOJ(g), 3".

HC-63A, Japan, 3".

Shepherd's Boy, Hum. 64
("The Good Shepherd")

Hum. 64 Shepherd's Boy, TMK-3.

HC-64A, USA(?), POP, no label, 5⅝".

53

Hum. 65 Farewell, TMK-6.

Farewell, Hum. 65
("So Long," "Goodbye," "Till We Meet Again")

Goebel's Hum. 65, Farewell, produced only with a round base and empty basket. Sizes listed over the years ranged from 4″ to 5½″ high. The pet lamb shown resting is a featured part of this figurine. Hummel copycats HC-65B and HC-65C are oval-based figurines without lamb. REL-65A is one of five different, religiously inspired figurines in this book. They all have "© 1947" incised on the edge of the bases and all bear religious messages. The REL-65A figurine is holding a sign that reads, "Delight Thyself in the Lord." I would be interested to know if other examples exist besides these. See PTR-65A, Planter section, for one Hummel-inspired Farewell planter.

HC-65A, USA(?), POP, no label, 4½″.

HC-65B, MIOJ(b), 4½″, no lamb.

HC-65C, MIOJ(b), 5⅝″, no lamb.

REL-65A, USA(?), POP, no label, 4½″. See discussion.

Key to Symbols

Hummel Copycat code: HC—Hummel copycat; HCM—mini-size; BE—bookend; BVS—bud vase; CDL—candleholder; MBX—music box; MC—Mel copycat; PLQ—plaque; PLQF—plaque figurine; PTR—planter; REL—religious message figurine; RMF—revolving musical figurine; SPS—salt and pepper shakers; TLP—table lamp; TPK—toothpick holder; WVS—wall vase. *Note:* Unless otherwise specified, all copycats pictured are made of ceramic.

Farm Boy, Hum. 66
("Three Pals," "Pig Boy," "Swineherd," "Happy-Go-Lucky Fellow")

This lad had many aliases, as noted, but he was only made in one 5″ size by Goebel since introduction in the late 1930s. Interestingly, the three Farm Boy Hummel copycats shown are all in the 5″ to 5¼″ size range. At first glance, the two POP figurines HC-66B and HC-66C look to be made from the same mold, but each has a different gold foil label affixed. HC-66B carries the D9 label and HC-66C has the D2 label. (See "How to Use This Book" section for label identification.) Not only are the labels different, the HC-66C figurine is far superior in workmanship to the other, even though both pieces are made from plaster-of-paris. See Beswick figurine No. 912, Farm Boy, in Beswick Hummel section.

Hum. 66 Farm Boy, TMK-5.

HC-66A, Taiwan(?), bisque, 5¼″.

HC-66B, USA, POP, D5 label, 5″.

HC-66C, USA, POP, D2 label, 5″.

55

Doll Mother, Hum. 67
("Little Doll Mother," "Little Mother of Dolls")

The much-loved Goebel Hum. 67, Doll Mother, was modeled in the late 1930s. It is always a popular baby shower gift and an affectionate and warmly appreciated Mother's Day gift. See PTR-67A, PTR-67B, and TPK-67A, Planter section, for two Hummel-inspired Doll Mother planters and one toothpick holder.

Hum. 67 Doll Mother,
TMK-5.

HC-67A, MIOJ(b), "American Children, Good Night" (r), 4⅝".

HC-67B, USA, POP, D2 label, 4⅜".

HC-67C, Japan(?), "Good Night," 4¾".

HC-67D, USA(?), POP, no label, 4½".

Lost Sheep, Hum. 68
("Shepherd's Boy")

The two Hummel copycats shown here rank above average. They possess good quality and detail as they relate to Goebel's Hum. 68, Lost Sheep, even though REL-68A is a POP figurine. HC-68A stands on a doughnut-style base. Either piece would represent a big plus in anyone's collection.

Hum. 68/2/0 Lost Sheep, TMK-5.

HC-68A, MIOJ(r), 4⅞".

REL-68A, USA(?), POP, no label, 5⅜". Incised edge of base "© 1947." Sign reads, "The Lord Is My Shepherd."

Happy Pastime, Hum. 69
("Knitter")

Happy Pastime, Goebel's Hum. 69, is my absolute favorite Hummel figurine. She is a great industrious kid. Knit one, purl two...or is it purl one, knit two? Whatever, Happy Pastime is the number one huggable Hummel in my life. So it was only natural for me to become a bit excited when I recently purchased the Occupied Japan HC-69A at a Utica, Michigan, antique show. It is a superior copy of Goebel's Hum. 69. She is color and detail correct, including the proper upward tilt of her head. She even has the forefinger of her left hand poking through the yarn just like her Goebel Hummel counterpart. See PTR-69A in Planter section for one Hummel-inspired Happy Pastime planter.

Hum. 69 Happy Pastime, TMK-5.

HC-69A, MIOJ(b), 3¾". Black bird.

HC-69B, USA, POP, D4 label, 3½". Blue bird.

HC-69C, USA, POP, D1 label, 3⅞". "MP" incised back of oval base. Blue bird.

HC-69D, Japan, 2¾". No bird.

HC-69E, USA(?), POP, no label, 3". Yellow bird.

Stormy Weather, Hum. 71
("Sunny Hours," "Under One Roof")

Stormy Weather, Hum. 71, originally modeled in the late 1930s, can be found in several variations in size and style. This popular Goebel Hummel figurine is equally prized when found as a copycat. The Occupied Japan HC-71C listed below with turquoise/blue umbrella is shown again in the Color Section along with another identical HC-71C, MIOJ(g), 5⅞" high, except umbrella is two-tone rust/tan. See a unique Stormy Weather table lamp in the Table Lamps section and Beswick figurine No. 908, Stormy Weather, in the Beswick Hummel section.

Hum. 71 Stormy Weather, TMK-3.

HC-71A, Japan(?), 5⅝". Marked "Rainin SH1C."

HC-71B, USA(?), POP, no label, 6¼". Unpainted.

HC-71C, MIOJ(g), 5⅞". Turquoise/blue umbrella variation.

HC-71D, USA, POP, D-7 label reads "Coventry Ware," 6½", cork-covered base.

Key to Symbols

Hummel Copycat code: HC—Hummel copycat; HCM—mini-size; BE—bookend; BVS—bud vase; CDL—candleholder; MBX—music box; MC—Mel copycat; PLQ—plaque; PLQF—plaque figurine; PTR—planter; REL—religious message figurine; RMF—revolving musical figurine; SPS—salt and pepper shakers; TLP—table lamp; TPK—toothpick holder; WVS—wall vase. *Note:* Unless otherwise specified, all copycats pictured are made of ceramic.

59

Little Gardener, Hum. 74

Originally designed with an oval base. Currently produced in a round base.

Hum. 74 Little Gardener, TMK-3.

HC-74A, Japan, marked "Sprinklin SH1D," Napco label, 5½", oval base. Excellent color, detail.

Globe Trotter, Hum. 79
('Happy Traveler," "Out into the Distance," "Stepping Out")

Globe Trotter, Hum. 79, was produced by Goebel in two distinct basket designs: the new style single weave and the old double weave version. All HC figurines on this page have the old style double weave baskets.

I initially discovered the three Hummel copycats HC-5B, similar to Goebel's Hum. 5 Strolling Along; HC-7E, similar to Goebel's Hum. 7 Merry Wanderer; and HC-79E, similar to Goebel's Hum. 79 Globe Trotter, advertised for sale in the United China & Glass Company's 1985 wholesale catalog and again in their 1986 catalog. They were listed as Item No. J19100, Porcelain Boy 7". They were sold as a three-piece set at a

Hum. 79 Globe Trotter, TMK-5.

HC-79A, Japan, 3¾" high.

HC-79B, USA, POP, D2 label, 5" high.

HC-79C, Japan, 4⅞" high.

Single weave

Double weave

Globe Trotter (continued)

wholesale price of $4.75 each figurine. This would place item in a $12 to $15 retail price range. Although this set become a favorite trio of mine, beware of the quality. F a collector's viewpoint you would be very fortunate to four good, acceptable pieces out of a dozen-piece carto purchased one dozen of each so I am writing from perso experience. As they say, "You only get what you pay fo

Many of the Globe Trotter style figurines lean to such an treme they almost fall off their base supports. The paint dec ration runs from hit-and-miss to fair and acceptable. Th again, these are not being produced for the discriminating co lector marketplace. In my opinion, the good examples are we worth the $15 each. Had the manufacturer paid more atten tion to production quality, we collectors would have some thing special. See Beswick figurine No. 913, Globe Trotter, i Beswick section.

HC-79D, MIOJ(b), 5⅞" high. Double-weave basket.

HC-79E, Taiwan, 6¾". Very good color and detail (except has oval base). Single-weave basket. See companion figurines HC-5B and HC-7E and Color Section.

chool Girl, Hum. 81
Primer Girl," "Little Scholar")

ebel's Hum. 81, School Girl, was produced in basically three
s: 4 ¼ ", 5", and 5 ½ ". The basket is empty in the two larg-
izes and full in the 81/2/0 4 ¼ " size. REL-81A has the
1947" copyright date incised back edge of base. Incised
ı base front is "Trust in the Lord." I purchased this figurine
ɔm John Hotchkiss, along with several other pieces, in Janu-
y 1983. This School Girl Hummel copycat was a full-page
ɔlor feature in his initial *Hummel Art* book on page 162. I
n always amazed to find a 1940s POP figurine that has
ıanaged to survive for so many years in near mint condition.
ee PLQF-81A, Plaque section, for Hummel copycat plaque fig-
ırine and BVS-81A, Planter section, for Hummel-inspired
School Girl bud vase.

Hum. 81/2/0 School
Girl, TMK-6.

REL-81A, USA(?), POP, no label, 5⅛". Empty
basket.

HC-81A, USA, POP, D2 label, 5". Empty
basket.

63

School Boy, Hum. 82
("Primer Boy," "Little Scholar," "School Boy Truant," "School Days")

The American Children figurine HC-82C was erroneously stamped in red "School Girl" underglaze. It would be interesting to locate an American Children "School Girl" figurine stamped "School Boy." The two would make a unique pair. See PLQF-82A, Plaque section, for Hummel copycat plaque figurine, and BVS-82A, Planter section, for Hummel-inspired School Boy bud vase.

Hum. 82/2/0 School Boy, TMK-3.

HC-82A, USA, POP, D2 label, 5".

HC-82B, USA(?), POP, no label, 5⅛".

HC-82C, OJ(b), "American Children"(r), erroneously marked "School Girl" (r), 5⅝".

HC-82D, Unknown origin, 4¾".

Key to Symbols

Hummel Copycat code: HC—Hummel copycat; HCM—mini-size; BE—bookend; BVS—bud vase; CDL—candleholder; MBX—music box; MC—Mel copycat; PLQ—plaque; PLQF—plaque figurine; PTR—planter; REL—religious message figurine; RMF—revolving musical figurine; SPS—salt and pepper shakers; TLP—table lamp; TPK—toothpick holder; WVS—wall vase. Note: Unless otherwise specified, all copycats pictured are made of ceramic.

(L to R) Top row: HC-16F, HC-17A, HC-13D, HC-47D, HC-47F.

Second row from top: HC-4A, HC-85E, HC-63A, HC-201B, HC-79B, HC-81A.

Third row: HC-65A, HC-69E, HC-69C, HC-69B, HC-5A.

Bottom row: HC-67B, HC-53A, HC-110A, HC-86B, HC-20A. All plaster-of-paris copycats.

(L to R) Top row: HC-89A, HC-64A, HC-56/AA, HC-15A, HC-15B.

Second row from top: HC-1A, HC-82B, HC-82A, HC-66B, HC-66C.

Third row: HC-57C, HC-57B, HC-112A, HC-21A, HC-94A.

Bottom row: HC-97A, HC-58D, HC-58B, HC-58C, HC-43A. All plaster-of-paris copycats.

(L to R) Top row: BVS-82A, BE-14/BA, BE-14/AA, BVS-81A.

Middle row: REL-68A, REL-81A, REL-65A, REL-95A, REL-5A.

Bottom row: HC-49F, HC-16D, HC-42A, HC-15C, HC-7B. All plaster-of-paris copycats.

(L to R) Top row: HC-97/98A, HC-67D, HC-95A, HC-95C, HC-98A.

Middle row: HC-4B, HC-16E, HC-82D, HC-95B, HC-97B, HC-7C.

Bottom row: TLP-47A, HC-89C, HC-2D, HC-47J. Ceramic and plaster-of-paris copycats.

(L to R) Top row:
HC-47H, HC-142A,
HC-131B, HC-184C,
HC-71A.

Second row from top:
CDL-54A, HC-86A,
HC-184A, HC-105A.

Third row: HC-13A,
HC-13C, HC-43B,
HC-127B, HC-79C,
HC-16A.

Bottom row: HC-67C,
HC-7D, HC-52A,
HC-130B, HC-47E. Ceramic
copycats.

(L to R) Top row: HC-5B,
HC-79E, HC-7E.

Middle row: HC-56/BA,
HC-141A, HC-142B,
HC-56/AB.

Bottom row: HC-194A,
HC-74A, HC-84A,
HC-83A, HC-23A. Ceram-
ic copycats.

(**L to R**) Top row: HC-119C, HC-50C, HC-50D, HC-143C.

Second row from top: HC-57A, HC-98D, HC-50A, HC-53B, HC-58A.

Third row: HC-49E, HC-49A, HC-49C, HC-94B.

Bottom row: HC-135B, HC-135A, HC-69D, HC-132C, HC-79A, HC-184B. Ceramic copycats.

(**L to R**) Top row: HC-127F, HC-98E, HC-66A, HC-87A, HC-129A.

Second row from top: HC-96A, HC-86C, HC-85D, HC-15D, SPS-239/CA, SPS-239/BA.

Third row: HC-344A, HC-342A, HC-195A.

Bottom row: HC-57D, HC-132B, HC-99A, HC-99C. Ceramic copycats.

(L to R) Top row: HC-1C, SPS-238/AA, HC-183A, SPS-238/CA, HC-85C.

Middle row: HC-109A, Hum. 40, HC-143B, HCM-143A, HC-63C, HC-128A.

Bottom row: HC-15E, HC-239/CB, HC-239/AA, HC-321A, HC-16C, HC-16B, HC-119B. Ceramic copycats.

(L to R) Top row: HC-85B, HC-7A, HC-111A, HC-124A, BE-14/AC.

Second row from top: HC-51A, HC-141B, HC-142C, HC-141C HC-201A.

Third row HC-197A, HC-47B, BE-14/AD, HC-86D, HC-131A.

Bottom row: PTR-67B, PTR-67A, PTR-307A, PTR-112A. Ceramic and plastic copycats.

(L to R) Top row:
PTR-14/BA, BE-16A,
PTR-47B.

Second row from top:
WVS-63A, BVS-47A,
PTR-119A, WVS-86A.

Third row: PTR-1E,
PTR-57A, PTR-1B, PTR-1D.

Bottom row: PTR-69A,
PTR-47A, PTR-1C,
PTR-63B, HC-89B. Ceramic
copycats.

Occupied Japan, TLP-71A.
See "Occupied Japan"
chapter and "Numerical
Photographic Section."

(L to R) Top row: amber, crystal, amethyst carnival, frosted.

Middle row: green, amberina, ruby, blue.

Bottom row: pastel blue, pastel green, frosted (red roses), and frosted (blue forget-me-nots). L. E. Smith glass goose girls. See "L. E. Smith Glass Company" chapter.

(L to R) Top row: HC-98B, HC-98C, HC-49D, HC-49B, HC-82C.

Middle row: HC-67A, HC-25B, HC-25A, HC-20B.

Bottom row: HC-13B, HC-71C, HC-85A, HC-71C, HC-119A. All Occupied Japan copycats. See "Occupied Japan" chapter and "Numerical Photographic Section."

Angel Serenade, Hum. 83
("Pious Melodies," "Psalmist," "Devout Tunes")

Hummel copycats do not come any better than the one shown here. In addition to many other similar features, note the chamfered corner base that matches Goebel Hummel bases in this style.

Hum. 83 Angel Serenade, TMK-2.

HC-83A, Japan(?), 5 ¾″. Excellent color, detail, and size.

Worship, Hum. 84
("At the Wayside," "Devotion")

HC-84A is a solemn but very exciting Hummel copycat possessing excellent color, detail, and size. This becomes quite obvious when it's seen praying beside Goebel's Hum. 84.

Hum. 84/0 Worship,
TMK-6.

HC-84A, Japan(?), 5½".

Serenade, Hum. 85
("The Flutist")

Note: Hat color usually black or grayish. Finger position either up or down.

Hum. 85/0 Serenade, TMK-2.

(L to R) HC-85A, MIOJ(b), 5¾"; HC-85B, Hong Kong, plastic, 5⅝", fingers up; HC-85C, Japan, 5⅜", marked "Flute Player SH1A," Napco label; HC-85D, Japan(?), 5"; HC-85E, USA, POP, D2 label, 4⅛", HC-85F, MIOJ(b), bisque, 4⅜".

Serenade Parade.

Happiness, Hum. 86
("Wandersong")

Goebel's Hum. 86, Happiness, can be found with rectangular or square base design. Happiness copycats have been made with rectangular, square, round, and oval designed bases as shown. See WVS-86A, Planter section, for one Hummel-inspired Happiness wall vase.

Hum. 86 Happiness, TMK-6.

HC-86A, Japan, marked "The Strummer SH1A," Napco (National Potteries, Cleveland, Ohio) label, 5¼", good color, detail, and size.

HC-86B, USA(?), POP, no label, 4¼".

HC-86C, Japan, marked "The Strummer S901," Napco (National Potteries, Cleveland, Ohio) label, 4".

HC-86D, Hong Kong, plastic, 4⅜".

HC-86E, MIOJ(b), bisque, 4".

For Father, Hum. 87
("Father's Joy")

Hum. 87 For Father, TMK-5.

HC-87A, Japan, 5⅜". Note oval versus round base.

Little Cellist, Hum. 89
("Musician")

Goebel's Hum. 89, Little Cellist, looked straight ahead in older models, similar to HC-89B, and were mounted on a square-cornered, rectangular base. He has since been restyled with a chamfered cornered, retangular base and is looking downward like HC-89A, HC-89C, and HC-89D are doing.

Hum. 89/I Little Cellist, TMK-5.

HC-89A, USA, POP, D2 label, 5¾".

HC-89B, Japan, 4½", formal attire.

HC-89C, USA(?), POP, no label, 7½".

HC-89D, MIOJ(b), 4⅝".

Surprise, Hum. 94
("What's Up?," "The Duet," "Hansel and Gretel")

Goebel's Surprise, Hum. 94, was introduced in 1938 and can be found in a range of sizes. Older models were produced with rectangular base. Some models have a base with chamfered corners similar to copycat HC-94C. Current models have oval bases. HC-94B is the smallest freestanding copycat I have ever come across. It is 1½″ high × 1″ wide. A tiny wire stub embedded in the center back of this figure protrudes outward. This wire and the lack of a common base lead me to believe that this piece was originally part of a larger Hummel look-alike in plastic, similar to Goebel's Heavenly Protection, Hum. 88. See RMF-94A and RMF-94B, Music Box section, for two Hummel Surprise-inspired revolving musical figurines.

Hum. 94/I Surprise, TMK-6.

HC-94A, USA(?), POP, no label, 5⅛″, oval base.

(L) HC-94B, Hong Kong, plastic, 1½″, freestanding. (R) HC-94C, Japan 4⅞″.

Hum. 95 Brother, TMK-3.

Brother, Hum. 95
("Village Hero," "Our Hero")

Goebel's Hum. 95, Brother, appears to be the same fellow used on Goebel's double figurine Hum. 94, Surprise. Brother, Hum. 95, was made in several color variations and slight changes may be found in suspenders. See HC-95C for a different suspender design compared to HC-95A, HC-95B, and REL-95A. See BE-95A and PLQF-95A, in Bookend and Plaque sections, for Hummel Brother-inspired bookend and plaque figurine.

HC-95A, USA(?), POP, no label, 5½″.

HC-95B, unknown origin, 4¾″.

HC-95C, USA, POP, D6 label, 5½″.

REL-95A, USA(?), POP, no label, 5¾″. Incised edge of base, "Jesus Never Fails © 1947."

Key to Symbols

Hummel Copycat code: HC—Hummel copycat; HCM—mini-size; BE—bookend; BVS—bud vase; CDL—candleholder; MBX—music box; MC—Mel copycat; PLQ—plaque; PLQF—plaque figurine; PTR—planter; REL—religious message figurine; RMF—revolving musical figurine; SPS—salt and pepper shakers; TLP—table lamp; TPK—toothpick holder; WVS—wall vase. *Note:* Unless otherwise specified, all copycats pictured are made of ceramic.

Little Shopper, Hum. 96
("Gretel," "Errand Girl," "Meg")

See PLQ-96A and PLQF-96A, Plaque section, for Little Shopper copycat figurine mounted plaque and plaque figurine. Also see PTR-96A in Planter section for one Hummel-inspired planter.

Hum. 96 Little Shopper, TMK-6.

HC-96A, Japan, 4¾".

Hum. 97 Trumpet Boy, TMK-6.

Trumpet Boy, Hum. 97
("The Little Musician")

Hum. 97, Trumpet Boy, usually produced by Goebel wearing a green jacket. All Hummel copycats shown here sport jackets in various shades of green. See PLQF-97A in Plaque section for one Hummel-inspired plaque-figurine. See Beswick Hummel No. 903, Trumpet Boy, in the Beswick section. This chap is also wearing a green jacket. HC-97/98A shows Trumpet Boy and Sister copycats, similar to Goebel's Hum. 97 and Hum. 98, mounted together on a common oval base. A unique combination with no known Goebel Hummel counterpart.

HC-97A, USA(?), POP, D4 label, 5⅛".

HC-97B, unknown origin, 4¾".

HC-97/98A, USA(?), POP, no label, 5⅜".

Sister, Hum. 98
("Little Shopper," "First Shopping")

See BE-98A and PLQF-98A, Bookend and Plaque sections, for Hummel-inspired Sister bookend and plaque figurine.

Hum. 98/0 Sister, TMK-3.

HC-98A, USA(?), POP, no label, 5⅜". Empty basket.

HC-98B, MIOJ(g), 5⅝". Bottle resting rear of basket.

83

HC-98C, MIOJ(b), 5¼″.
Bottle resting rear of basket.

HC-98D, Japan(?), 5″. Empty basket.

HC-98E, Japan(?), 5½″. Bottle resting front
of basket. Not usually found with this bottle position.

84

Eventide, Hum. 99

Eventide, Hum. 99, is believed to be adapted from Wayside Devotion, Hum. 28, except without shrine. Here are three good examples of copycats and/or Hummel-inspired figurines that are incomplete when compared to Goebel's Hum. 99, Eventide. It is unknown whether the manufacturer was trying to circumvent Goebel's copyright protection or just teasing the copyright system. With the exception of no lambs and the exclusion of one lamb in HC-99C, the three pieces have a lot in common with their Goebel Hummel counterpart.

Hum. 99 Eventide, TMK-2.

HC-99A, Japan(?), 4″. No lambs.

HC-99B, MIOJ(r), 3⅞″. No lambs.

HC-99C, Japan, 4¼″. One lamb.

85

Adoration with Bird, Hum. 105
("Bird Lovers")

Hum. 105 was listed by Goebel as a Closed Edition in 1935. The very few known examples are considered to be quite rare. Hum. 105 looks to be an adaptation of Goebel's Hum. 23, Adoration. Locating a copycat of this rare figurine is very rewarding, even though the manufacturer did add a dog to the family. All other aspects of this HC group are excellent, with the usual exception of its lacking the high quality possessed only by its ⅜" taller M.I. Hummel counterpart.

Happy Traveller, Hum. 109
("Wanderer," "Out in Far Places")

Hum. 105 Adoration with Bird, very rare, TMK-1. Robert L. Miller collection.

Hum. 109/0 Happy Traveller, TMK-3.

HC-105A, Japan(?), 4⅜". Rectangular base is 3⅜" w × 2" d. Note addition of dog.

HC-109A, Japan(?), 5½".

Let's Sing, Hum. 110
("Heini, the Accordion Player")

Wayside Harmony, Hum. 111
("Duet," "Fence Duet," "Boy on Fence," "Boy Just Resting," "Just Sittin' Boy," "Father's Cleverest")

Hum. 110/0 Let's Sing, TMK-2.

Hum. 111/I Wayside Harmony, TMK-5.

HC-110A, USA(?), POP, D4 label, 4⅛″. Bird location not correct.

HC-111A, Taiwan, 5⅞″. Modern Alpine style.

Just Resting, Hum. 112
("Girl on Fence," "Girl Just Resting," "Just Sittin' Girl,"
"Mother's Most Beloved")

See PTR-112A, Planters section, for one Hummel inspired, Just
Resting planter.

Hum. 112/3/0 Just Rest-
ing, TMK-6.

HC-112A, USA, POP, D2 label, 5″.

Heavenly Song, Candleholder, Hum. 113

CDL-113A is a rare copycat of the rare Hum. 113. I located this piece at a weekend Park 'n' Swap in Phoenix, Arizona, November 1986. The previous owner stated that it had been in her family over thirty years. Goebel's Hum. 113 is often confused with Hum. 31 and Hum. 54.

Hum. 113 Heavenly Song, Candleholder, currently discontinued, scarce, TMK-1. Robert L. Miller collection.

HC-113A, unknown origin, alabaster, 3⅜" h × 4½" w, with green felt covered base.

Postman, Hum. 119
("Special Messenger")

HC-119A is one of those better quality, Occupied Japan, Hummel copycats with good color, detail, and size. Although there is no Hummel parallel, notice the excellent detail shown on the PTR-119A Hummel-inspired Postman planter. Goebel's Postman, Hum. 119, is a very popular M. I. Hummel collectible.

Hum. 119 Postman, TMK-2.

HC-119A, MIOJ(b), 5⅝". Marked with script "KW" in blue capital letters underglaze.

PTR-119A, Japan(?), 4" h × 5¼" w × 3½" d. Marked "Mailman SH721." A quality planter.

HC-119B, Japan(?), 5⅜". Marked "The Mailman." No bow tie.

HC-119C, Japan(?), 5⅞". I call this "Postman and Friend." No Hummel counterpart known.

Hello, Hum. 124
("Chef Hello," "The Boss")

Hum. 124/0 Hello, TMK-3.

HC-124A, Hong Kong, plastic, 5⅝″.

Hum. 127 Doctor, TMK-3.

Doctor, Hum. 127
("Doll Doctor")

Note the incorrect doll position of copycats HC-127B, HC-127D, and HC-127E.

HC-127A, OJ(b), "American Children, The Doctor," (r), 5″. Florence Archambault collection.

HC-127B, Japan, 4⅞″. Doll position reversed.

HC-127C, Japan(?), 4¼″. Marked "Little Doc."

HC-127D, MIOJ(r), 4⅞″. Doll position reversed.

HC-127E, MIOJ(b), 5¾″. Doll position reversed.

HC-127F, Japan (?), 5⅜″, marked "Little Doc SHIE." Note trousers.

Baker, Hum. 128
("Little Confectioner")

This little confectioner looks to be sampling his Gugelhupf Bavarian pound cake.

Hum. 128 Baker, TMK-5.

HC-128A, Japan, "American Children, Little Cook 363" (b), 5¼".
Silver-on-red foil label reads, "Leftons Exclusives Japan."

Band Leader, Hum. 129
("Leader")

Hum. 129 Band Leader,
TMK-1.

HC-129A, Japan(?), 6″. Marked "Maestro SH1A."

94

Duet, Hum. 130
("Singing Pair," "The Songsters")

Hum. 130 Duet, TMK-1.

HC-130A, Japan(?), 11⅛". Marked "Duet SH544C." Rue Dee Marker collection.

HC-130B, Japan(?), 5¼". Both singers wearing bow ties.

95

Street Singer, Hum. 131
("Singer," "Soloist," "Chamber Singer")

Hum. 131 Street Singer,
TMK-1.

HC-131A, Hong Kong, plastic, 5″. No printed music notes.

HC-131B, Japan, 5½″.

Star Gazer, Hum. 132

Hum. 132 Star Gazer, TMK-6.

(L) HC-132A, OJ(b), "American Children, Little Astrologer" (r), 4¼", Florence Archambault collection. (R) HCM-132A, Japan(?), 2½", mini-sized.

HC-132B, Japan(?), 3⅞". Marked "Little Astrologer."

Key to Symbols

Hummel Copycat code: HC—Hummel copycat; HCM—mini-size; BE—bookend; BVS—bud vase; CDL—candleholder; MBX—music box; MC—Mel copycat; PLQ—plaque; PLQF—plaque figurine; PTR—planter; REL—religious message figurine; RMF—revolving musical figurine; SPS—salt and pepper shakers; TLP—table lamp; TPK—toothpick holder; WVS—wall vase. *Note:* Unless otherwise specified, all copycats pictured are made of ceramic.

HC-132C, Japan(?), 4⅜". Marked "Little Astrologer."

Soloist, Hum. 135
("High Tenor")

See RMF-135A in Revolving Musical Figurines section for one Hummel Soloist-inspired revolving musical figurine.

Hum. 135 Soloist, TMK-5.

(L) HC-135A, Japan(?), 3⅞". Marked "Musician Singing." (R) HC-135B, Japan, 5".

Apple Tree Girl, Hum. 141
("Spring")

Goebel's Hum. 141, Apple Tree Girl, was produced in size range from a small 4″ without bird in tree to a very large 32″. Hummel copycats HC-141A and 141B depict the old-style brown base that appeared to become part of the tree trunk itself.

Hum. 141/I Apple Tree Girl, TMK-5.

HC-141B, Hong Kong, plastic, 4⅛″. Minus bird.

HC-141A, Japan(?), 6¼″. Marked "Romance SH3C." Made without bird.

HC-141C, Hong Kong, plastic, 4⅛″. Minus bird.

Hum. 142/I Apple Tree
Boy, TMK-5.

Apple Tree Boy, Hum. 142
("Fall")

Goebel's Hum. 142, Apple Tree Boy, like its companion piece, Hum. 141, Apple Tree Girl, was produced in several sizes from a small 4″ without bird in tree, to a very large 30″ figurine. Copycat HC-142B depicts the old-style brown tapered base.

HC-142B, Japan, Napco label, 6⅛″. Minus bird.

HC-142C, Hong Kong, plastic, 4⅛″. Minus bird.

HC-142A, Japan, 6¼″.

Boots, Hum. 143
("Shoemaker")

Note the detail of the boy of Hummel copycat HC-143B, paired with his little sister helper on a round common base. There is no known Goebel Hummel counterpart to this double figurine, nor is there a Hummel parallel to the little sister helper. What makes this HC figurine unique is the boy, himself, when you compare him to Sister Hummel's drawing. The creator of HC-143B removed the shoes held in the boy's left hand and passed them on to the girl to clutch. Obvious similarities, such as striped shirts and trousers; the horizontal position of the boots with their individual pull straps; the outward thrust of the shirt collar tips; cut of the aprons; the cowlick disarray of hair; and, finally, the identical finger and thumb positions of the right hands, invite conjecture. Could this be an unlicensed original figurine?

Hum. 143/0 Boots, TMK-3.

(L) HCM-143A, Japan(?), 3", mini-sized. (R) HC-143A, Japan(b), "American Children, Shoe Maker"(b), 5⅝".

Reproduction of Sister Hummel drawing in form of a 5½" × 4" folded notecard No. 10 H 266 printed, published, and copyrighted in the U.S. in 1941 by Ars Sacra, Herbert Dubler, Inc. Carol Lucas collection.

HC-143B, Japan, 6". Silver on blue foil label "Royal Sealy Japan."

Umbrella Boy, Hum. 152/A
("In Safety," "Boy under Roof," "Boy under Umbrella")

See BE-152/AA in Bookend section for Hummel-inspired Umbrella Boy bookend.

Umbrella Girl, Hum. 152/B
("In Safety," "Girl under Roof," "Girl under Umbrella")

See BE-152/BA in Bookend section for Hummel-inspired Umbrella Girl bookend.

Hum. 152/0/A Umbrella Boy, TMK-6.

Hum. 152/0/B Umbrella Girl, TMK-6.

HC-152/AA, Spain, Popware, 5", red felt covered base.

HC-152/BA, Spain, Popware, 4⅞", red felt covered base.

She Loves Me, She Loves Me Not, Hum. 174
("Boy Sitting Before Fence")

See BE-251/BA She Loves Me, She Loves Me Not bookend.

Hum. 174 She Loves Me, She Loves Me Not, eyes down, TMK-6.

HC-174A, Spain, Popware, 4″, red felt covered base.

Good Friends, Hum. 182
("Friends," "Girl with Kid")

See BE-251/AA Good Friends bookend.

Hum. 176/0 Happy Birthday, TMK-6.

Hum. 182 Good Friends, TMK-1.

HC-176A, Japan(?), 5⅛", good color, detail, and size. John Martin collection.

HC-182A, Spain, Popware, 4", red felt covered base.

(L to R) Top row: HC-314A, HC-68A, HC-57E, HC-47C, HC-47A.

Middle row: HC-65C, HC-50B, HC-127D, HC-127A, HC-127E.

Bottom row: HC-217A, HC-65B, HC-16H, HC-89D, HC-132A. All Occupied Japan copycats. See "Occupied Japan" chapter and "Numerical Photographic Section."

(L to R) Top row: HC-2B, HC-2C, HC2A, HC-1D, HC-1B, HC-1E.

Second row from top: HC-85F, PTR-1A, PTR-239/CA, PTR-20A, HC-99B.

Third row: HC-53C, HC-239/BA, HC-238/AB, HC-238/BB, HC-238/CB, HC-239/CA, HC-69A.

Bottom row: SPS-2A, SPS-239/AA, SPS-239/AB, SPS-239/CB, SPS-239/AC, SPS-16A, SPS-239/BB, SPS-239/CC. All Occupied Japan copycats. See "Occupied Japan" chapter and "Numerical Photographic Section."

(L to R) Top row: HC-5C, CDL-38A, CDL-39A, CDL-40A, HC-63B, HC-86E, HC-317A.

Middle row: HC-79D, PTR-65A, PTR-96A, PTR-63A, PTR-13A.

Bottom row: BE-14/BB, TPK-67A, TPK-51A, BE-14/AB. All Occupied Japan copycats. See "Occupied Japan" chapter and "Numerical Photographic Section."

(L to R) Top row: Dubler's Boy with Tuba, Boy with Saxophone, Boy with Drum, Boy with Flute, and Band Leader. All unnumbered.

Middle row: Dubler's No. 38 Little Chemist, No. 31 Little Skipper, No. 39 Sleepy Baby, No. 32 Little Bookworm, and No. 40 Mother's Helper.

Bottom row: Dubler's No. 37 Doll's Doctor, No. 46 Angel's Song, No. 45 Madonna and Child, No. 34 Little Mother, plain apron, and No. 34 Little Mother, decorated apron. Full details will be found in the Dubler Figurines chapter.

(**L to R**) Top row: Dubler's No. 59 Billy Birthday, No. 43 Cactus Puss, No. 41 Hello! Birdie, and No. 44 Bawling Bennie.

Middle row: Dubler's No. 36 Little Cobbler, Decorative Figurines' unnumbered Country Boy, and No. 25 Hello Darling Boy wall plaque. Dubler's No. 48 Dentist Dodger and No. 35 Little Mailman.

Bottom row: Dubler's unnumbered Girl on Apple Tree wall plaque, unnumbered Boy on Apple Tree wall plaque, and unnumbered Spring Song Girl wall plaque. For full details see chapters on Dubler and the Decorative Figurines Corp.

(L to R) Top row: BE-61/AA, HC-174A, BE-61/BA.

Middle row: BE-60/AA, HC-182A, BE-60/BA.

Bottom row: BE-152/AA, Beswick 903, BE-152/BA. See Spanish Hummel copycats and "Numerical Photographic Section."

(**L to R**) Top row: HC-152/AA, HC-59A, HC-152/BA.

Middle row: BE-251/BA, MC-6A, BE-251/AA.

Bottom row: BE-95A, HC-28A, BE-98A. See Spanish Hummel copycats and "Numerical Photographic section."

(**L to R**) Top row: RMF-94A, RMF-336A, RMF-94B.

Middle row: MBX-57A, RMF-218A, MBX-58A.

Bottom row: RMF-17A, RMF-135A, RMF-7A. For full details see "Music Boxes, Revolving Musical Figurines" chapter. All of the Hummel copycats appearing in this Color Section are pictured elsewhere in the book in black-and-white with accompanying text that provides full particulars about each. Refer to the "Numerical Photographic Section" by copycat number and/or to the specific chapter where indicated.

Forest Shrine, Hum. 183

("Doe at Shrine")

HC-183A, Japan(?), bisque, 6".

Hum. 183 Forest Shrine, TMK-5.

Latest News, Hum. 184

At one time, Goebel's Hum. 184, Latest News, was made with an untitled newspaper, allowing factory visitors to select a title. Some would use the name of their favorite hometown paper. Consequently, many names can be found. Copycats HC-184A and HC-184C are shown mounted on the old style square base. HC-184B has the new round base. HC-184C, like its old-style Hummel counterpart, is shown with boy's eyes looking over top of newspaper; whereas, Goebel's new model has boy's eyes looking down.

Hum. 184 Latest News, TMK-5.

HC-184A, Japan, Napco label, 5". Marked "News SH3C." "Müncbener Presse" newspaper.

HC-184B, Japan, 3⅞". Newspaper untitled.

HC-184C, Japan, "American Children, News 363"(b), 5¼". Silver-on-red foil label reads, "Leftons Exclusives Japan." "Daily Mail" newspaper.

Watchful Angel, Hum. 194
("Guardian Angel," Angelic Care")

Hum. 194 Watchful Angel, TMK-4. Robert L. Miller collection.

HC-194A, Japan, 5¾".

Barnyard Hero, Hum. 195

Be Patient, Hum. 197
("Little Duckling Mother," "Mother of Ducks")

Hum. 195/2/0 Barnyard
Hero, TMK-5.

Hum. 197/2/0 Be Pa-
tient, TMK-3.

HC-195A, Taiwan, bisque, 5".

HC-197A, Hong Kong, plastic, 4¼".

Hum. 201 Retreat to Safety, TMK-1.

Retreat to Safety, Hum. 201
("Afraid")

The Hummel copycat HC-201A is a very obvious copy of Goebel's Retreat to Safety, Hum. 201. The figurine HC-201B is, perhaps, another story. The notecard 10 H 4782, by Ars Sacra, Herbert Dubler, Inc., with the printed notation, "A brave young man," pictured, features a drawing by Sister Hummel. It appears to me that this figurine is an adaptation made directly from this Hummel drawing and not a copy of Goebel's Hum. 201. My conclusions are based on the way the fence is constructed with extra long post resting against boy's backside and by the overall design of the fence in general. Note the way the ground rises to a mound slightly engulfing the short post on the left in very good adaptation of these two elements from Sister Hummel's drawing. Two areas where this HC figurine falls short are the missing neckware and the incorrect position of the boy's hands, which are resting on each side of top rail as in the old style Goebel Hum. 201, Retreat to Safety. If this were a direct adaptation from Sister Hummel's artwork, then I ask, "Is this an unauthorized genuine Hummel figurine?" It is the reader's decision — M. I. Hummel or am I not?

HC-201A, Hong Kong, plastic, 3¾". Gold foil label "Deutschland."

HC-201B, USA, POP, D2, label, 4⅞".

A brave young man

Reproduction of Sister Hummel drawing on notecard 10 H 4782, Ars Sacra, Herbert Dubler, Inc., "A brave young man © 1942."

Boy with Toothache, Hum. 217
("Toothache," "At the Dentist")

Boy with Toothache, Hum. 217, is another instance where the master sculptor working at W. Goebel Porzellanfabrik in Rodenthal has taken some artistic liberties in the transformation of Sister Hummel's drawing into a figurine. It is obvious when viewing her work in notecard form as it relates to Goebel's Hum. 217 that some detail was left behind. But, as always, the love of Sister Hummel's children transcends, and I feel and share the boy's deep concern of his impending fate. According to *Hotchkiss' Handbook to Hummel Art*, "There are two known copies of this drawing. Sister Hummel made a second one for her dentist in Saulgau."

Hum. 217 Boy with Toothache, TMK-5.

Now study the Occupied Japan, American Children rendition marked "Toothache." If one were to remove the boy's best friend and the flower bed atop the figurine's base, what remains is a much more accurate adaptation of Sister Hummel's drawing. Note the detail of the boy pulling the bellcord at the dentist's office signaling, "Let's get it over with." HC-217A and HCM-217A are not copies of Goebel's Hum. 217, but seem to be unauthorized adaptations taken from her artwork. You be the judge — M. I. Hummel or am I not?

(L) HC-217A, OJ(b), "American Children, Toothache" (b), 5½". Sign attached to bellcord reads, "Dentist Dr." (R) HCM-217A, Japan(?), 3¼", mini-sized, same sign.

Reproduction of Sister Hummel drawing in form of 5½" × 4" folded notecard No. 10 H 5552, printed, published, and copyrighted in the U.S. in 1946 by Ars Sacra, Herbert Dubler, Inc., New York.

Angel Trio (B) Set, Hum. 238

(Sold separately as: Angel with Lute, Hum. 238A; Angel with Accordion, Hum. 238B; Angel with Trumpet, Hum. 238C.)

Hummel copycats HC-238/AB, HC-238/BB, and HC-238/CB are included here with erroneous intent. This group is clearly marked "Made in Occupied Japan," which dates them in the 1947 era, twenty years prior to Goebel's 1967 Angel Trio copyright date. Although their wings and musical instruments are out of position when compared to their Hummel counterparts, they do comprise an interesting assembly. I call them the "Swinging Angel Trio." This set was possibly inspired by Goebel's Hum. 38, Hum. 39, and Hum. 40, Candleholder series, but without candle sockets. See SPS-238/AA, SPS-238/CA, Salt and Pepper Shakers section, for one pair Angel Trio (B) salt and pepper shakers.

Hum. 238/A, B, C Angel Trio (B) Set, TMK-6.

(L to R) HC-238/AA, Japan(?), 2¼″; HC-238/BA, Japan(?), 2″; HC-238/CA, Japan(?), 2¼″.

(L to R) HC-238/AB, MIOJ(b); HC-238/BB, MIOJ(b); HC-238/CB, MIOJ(r). All 2⅛″.

(L to R) HC-238/AC, Japan(?), 2¼″; HC-238/BC, Japan(?), 2″; HC-238/CC, Japan(?), 2¼″.

Children Trio (A) (Set), Hum. 239

I had to combine three figurines from the two sets of figurines shown to complete one set of Hummel copycats. At best, this is a stretch Hummel ragamuffin group that shouldn't even be compared to Goebel's Children Trio (A) (Set), Hum. 239, but I did so anyway. See PTR-239/CA, Planter section, for a Hummel-inspired planter. See the following in the Salt and Pepper Shaker section for Hummel-inspired salt and pepper shaker sets: SPS-239/AA, 239/AB, 239/AC, 239/BA, 239/BB, 239/CA, 239/CB, and 239/CC.

Hum. 239/A, B, C Children Trio (A) Set.
239/A Girl with Nosegay, TMK-6.
239/B Girl with Doll, TMK-6.
239/C Boy with Horse, TMK-6.

(L) HC-239/BA, MIOJ(b), 3⅛". **(R)** HC-239/CA, MIOJ(b), 3⅛".

(L to R) HC-239/AA, HC-239/BA, HC-239/CB.

(L) HC-239/AA, Japan 3⅛".
(R) HC-239/CB, Japan, 3⅛".

Good Friends, Bookend, Hum. 251/A

Both wooden bookends are 5¼"h × 4"w × 4¼"d, with red felt covered bases. See Spanish Hummel section for detailed discussion.

She Loves Me, She Loves Me Not, Bookend, Hum. 251/B

Hum. 251/A Good Friends, Bookend, TMK-3. Robert L. Miller collection.

Hum. 251/B She Loves Me, She Loves Me Not, Bookend, TMK-3. Robert L. Miller collection.

BE-251/AA, Spain, Popware figurine is 3¾" high.

BE-251/BA, Spain, Popware figurine, 4" high.

120

Confidentially, Hum. 314
("Dialogue")

Not for You, Hum. 317
("Nothing for You")

Hum. 314 Confidential-
ly (new style), TMK-6.

Hum. 317 Not for You,
TMK-6.

HC-314A, OJ(b), "American Children, Just
a Cactus" (r), 5½". More modern version.

HC-317A, MIOJ(r), 5¼". No dog.

Hum. 321 Wash Day, TMK-4.

Wash Day, Hum. 321
("Big Wash")

I will condense my comparisons and comments and just say that Hummel copycat HC-321A retains more of the drawing's elements in its transition to a figurine than Goebel's Hum. 321, Wash Day does when both are compared to Sister Hummel's original. Particularly note that the copycat retains the two clothes posts with flowers. Compare the relative size of the clothes hanging out to dry—the sheet of the copycat figurine as opposed to the pantaloons being hung out in Sister Hummel's drawing. In conclusion, M.I. Hummel or am I not?

HC-321A, Japan(?), 5⅝". Marked "Monday Wash S296C."

Reproduction of Sister Hummel drawing on notecard No. 10 H 261, Ars Sacra, Herbert Dubler, Inc., © 1941. Printed and copyrighted in the U.S.

Mischief Maker, Hum. 342

Feathered Friends, Hum. 344
("Swan Pond")

Hum. 342 Mischief Maker, TMK-6.

Hum. 344 Feathered Friends, TMK-6.

HC-342A, Taiwan, bisque, 4⅞".

HC-344A, Taiwan, bisque, 4⅝".

Other Bookends

Although this pair has no Goebel Hummel counterpart as bookends, the figurines themselves do. Both figurines show excellent color, detail, and size when compared to Goebel's Hum. 95, Brother, and Hum. 98, Sister. These two probably date from the late 1930s or early 1940s as attested by a similar 1937 vintage pair featured on page 211 of Hotchkiss' book *Hummel Art II*. BE-95A and BE-98A are better quality plaster-

Hum. 95 Brother, TMK-3.

Hum. 98/0 Sister, TMK-3.

BE-95A, USA(?), POP, no label. Figurine, 4¾". Bookend, 5⅞" h × 3¾" w × 4⅛" d, with brown felt covered base.

BE-98A, USA(?), POP, no label. Figurine, 5". Bookend, 6" h × 3¾" w × 4¼" d, with brown felt covered base.

of-paris items that are in very good condition. (See Miles Kimball catalog photograph of bookends possibly from same manufacturer.) I credit tender loving care for the longevity of both and their survival as a twosome. See Index for other bookends.

Hum. 152/0/A Umbrella
Boy, TMK-6.

Hum. 152/0/B Umbrella
Girl, TMK-6.

Both wooden bookends are 5⅞"h × 4½"w × 5⅝"d, with red felt covered bases.

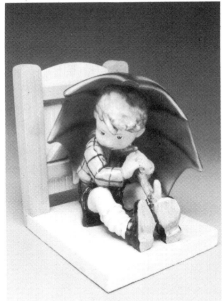

BE-152/AA, Spain, Popware figurine, 5".

BE-152/BA, Spain, Popware figurine, 4⅞".

Planters, Bud and Wall Vases, Toothpick Holders, Salt and Pepper Shakers

Hummel-inspired planters, bud and wall vases, toothpick holders, and salt and pepper shakers are something special to find. It takes a keen eye for Hummel detail and a good basic knowledge of the M. I. Hummel line to spot these elusive collectibles. They are cataloged here as Hummel-inspired, because there are no known Hummel counterparts in the form of planters, toothpick holders, etcetera. The term Hummel hybrid would be more descriptive, if not all-encompassing, for this class of collectible. These hybrids consist of Goebel Hummel figurine designs that have been separated and rearranged to the extent that they travel incognito from garage sales to flea markets to antique shows around the country without being readily identifiable, although they still possess some form of the M. I. Hummel mystique. All were cleverly conceived to conceal their true identity, although, in most cases, the main Hummel theme of that particular figurine endures. All the Puppy Love planters have five items in common, i.e., hat, umbrella, purse, violin, and puppy. Planter PTR-1C has the boy seated rather than standing, but the Puppy Love design remains. PTR-13A Meditation has a

planter receptacle in place of her basket. Two very desirable planters are PTR-119A Postman, shown earlier with Goebel's Hum. 119 discussion, and PTR-20A Prayer Before Battle.

It is extremely interesting to note the variety of these Hummel-inspired pieces and to realize how they relate to the Goebel Hummel figurine derivatives. Not one has been found that could be classified as an adaptation of one of Sister Hummel's drawings. They all appear to be directly inspired by Goebel's M. I. Hummel creations. Hummel collectors should be intrigued as they thumb through the following pages, closely examining the twenty-eight planters, bud and wall vases, and toothpick holders, plus the dozen salt and pepper shakers. Since the examples shown have no known Hummel parallels, I have shown the M. I. Hummel figurine, for ease of detail comparison, that possibly inspired the manufacturer. No M. I. Hummel figurines are shown with the salt and pepper shakers for comparison. Just compare the SPS number with Goebel's Hum. number, i.e., SPS-238/AA would be compared with Hum. 238/A shown earlier in this book.

Hum. 1 Puppy Love, TMK-6.

PTR-1A, Puppy Love planter, MIOJ(b), 2¾″ h × 2½″ w × 1½″ d.

PTR-1B Puppy Love planter, Japan, 3¼″ h × 4⅛″ w × 3⅛″ d.

PTR-1D Puppy Love planter, Japan, 5¼" h × 3⅞" w × 3" d.

PTR-1E Puppy Love planter, Japan, 5¼" h × 3⅞" w × 3" d.

PTR-1C Puppy Love planter, Japan, 2⅞" h × 3" w × 2⅛" d.

Hum. 13/0 Meditation, TMK-3.

PTR-13A Meditation planter, MIOJ(r), 5⅛" h × 4¼" w × 2⅝" d.

Planters, etc. (continued)

Although obviously a planter, this PTR-14/BA was paralleled with Goebel's Hum. 14/B bookend due to the flatness of the girl's back to which the planter receptacle is attached. If the planter portion were removed, she would serve as a perfect bookend. In addition, this piece can be weighted with sand, as can Hum. 14/B, through a large hole in the bottom of the figurine, then sealed with a stopper. This could be used as a combination planter/bookend. I was told there was a companion bookworm boy planter that was severely broken and discarded.

Hum. 14/B Book Worm Bookend, TMK-3.

PTR-14/BA Book Worm planter, Japan(?), 5⅝" h × 3⅞" w × 7" d.

Hum. 20 Prayer Before Battle, TMK-2.

PTR-20A Prayer Before Battle planter, MIOJ(b), 2⅞" h × 2½" w × 1½" d.

Hum. 47/0 Goose Girl, TMK-5.

PTR-47B Goose Girl planter, Japan, 5¾" h × 4⅛" w × 3⅝" d.

PTR-47A Goose Girl planter, Japan(?), 3" h × 3" w × 2¼" d.

BVS-47A Goose Girl bud vase, Japan 5⅛" h × 3¾" w × 1⅝" d.

Planters, etc. (continued)

Hum. 51/0 Village Boy, TMK-3.

TPK-51A Village Boy toothpick holder, MIOJ(b), 4⅜″h × 3½″ w × 2⅜″d.

Hum. 57/1 Chick Girl, TMK-6.

PTR-57A Chick Girl "Wishing Well" planter, Japan, 4½″h × 3½″ w × 3″d.

Hum. 63 Singing Lesson, TMK-6.

PTR-63A Singing Lesson planter, MIOJ(g), 3½"h × 3" w × 2⅜"d.

PTR-63B Singing Lesson planter, Japan, 2⅞"h × 3" w × 2⅜"d.

WVS-63A Singing Lesson wall vase, Japan, 5¼"h × 3" w × 1⅜"d.

Planters, etc. (continued)

Hum. 65 Farewell, TMK-6.

PTR-65A Farewell planter, MIOJ(g), 3¼"h × 3½" w × 3"d.

Hum. 67 Doll Mother, TMK-5.

PTR-67A Doll Mother planter, Japan, 3½"h × 3⅛" w × 3"d.

PTR-67B Doll Mother planter, Japan(?), 4⅞"h × 4⅞" w × 3⅜"d.

TPK-67A Doll Mother toothpick holder, MIOJ(b), 4½"h × 3" w × 2⅜"d.

Hum. 69 Happy Pastime, TMK-5.

PTR-69A Happy Pastime planter, Japan, 4"h × 3¾" w × 3½"d.

Planters, etc. (continued)

The bud vases shown in photos BVS-81A and BVS-82A have a glass vial insert 1″ in diameter by 3⅛ ″ high for holding fresh flowers and water.

Hum. 81/2/0 School Girl, TMK-6.

BVS-81A School Girl bud vase, USA, POP, D7 label reads "Coventry Ware," 5⅛″h × 4⅜″ w × 2¼″d, cork-covered base.

Hum. 82/2/0 School Boy, TMK-3.

BVS-82A School Boy bud vase, USA, POP, D7 label reads "Coventry Ware," 5″h × 4⅜″ w × 2¾″d, cork-covered base.

Hum. 86 Happiness,
TMK-6.

WVS-86A Happiness wall vase, Japan,
5¼"h × 3" w × 1¼"d.

Hum. 96 Little Shopper,
TMK-6.

PTR-96A Little Shopper planter, MIOJ(g),
4"h × 2¾" w × 3"d.

Hum. 112/3/0 Just Resting, TMK-6.

PTR-112A Just Resting planter, Japan, 4⅜"h × 4¾" w × 2⅞"d.

Hum. 239/C Boy with Horse, TMK-6.

PTR-239/CA Boy with Horse planter, MIOJ(b), 3¼"h × 2⅞" w × 1⅜"d.

Hum. 307 Good Hunting, TMK-6.

PTR-307A Good Hunting planter, Japan, 3"h × 2⅞" w × 2½"d.

Salt and Pepper Shakers

With the exception of Hummel copycats SPS-238/AA, SPS-238/CA, and SPS-2A, the rest of the salt and pepper shaker figurine groupings shown here should be classified as stretch Hummels. Boy with horse shows possibilities as does girl with doll. Girl with nosegay is difficult to accept even as a stretch Hummel—so just call her Hummel-inspired. An interesting collection, nonetheless, particularly considering that eight out of the twelve pieces shown are marked "Made in Occupied Japan."

(L) SPS-238/AA, Japan, Angel with Lute, 2¼". **(R)** SPS-238/CA, Japan, Angel with Trumpet, 2".

(L) SPS-2A, MIOJ(r), Little Fiddler, no umbrella, 4⅜". **(R)** SPS-239/AA, MIOJ(b), Girl with Nosegay, 4⅜".

(L) SPS-239/BA, Japan, bisque, Girl with Doll, 4¼". **(R)** SPS-239/CA, Japan, bisque, Boy with Horse, 4½".

(L) SPS-239/AB, MIOJ(r), Girl with Nosegay and basket, 4¼". **(R)** SPS-239/CB, MIOJ(r), Boy with Horse, 4⅜".

137

Salt and Pepper Shakers (continued)

(L) SPS-239/AC, MIOJ(b), Girl with Nose-gay and basket, 4⅜". **(R)** SPS-16A, MIOJ(b), Little Hiker, 4⅜".

(L) SPS-239/BB, MIOJ(b), Girl with Doll, 4¼". **(R)** SPS-239/CC, MIOJ(b), Boy with Horse, 4⅜".

Plaque and Plaque Figurines

The USA(?), POP, plaque figurines in this section range in size from 3¾" to 4⅜" high. Backs of figurines are flat and are mounted under an oval shaped convex glass dome as shown in photograph PLQ-96A. This particular plaque is 8" high × 4" wide with a 4" figurine similar to "Little Shopper" mounted inside. See

Hotchkiss' *Hummel Art II*, page 212, for another plaque of the same design displaying the Hummel copycat figurine "Brother." Without some type of proof, I cannot credit Herbert Dubler, Inc., with the manufacture and/or distribution of these collectibles.

PLQF-81A, similar to Hum. 81 School Girl.

PLQF-82A, similar to Hum. 82 School Boy.

PLQF-95A, similar to Hum. 95 Brother.

PLQ-96A, similar to Hum. 96 Little Shopper. See discussion.

PLQF-96A, similar to Hum. 96 Little Shopper.

PLQF-97A, similar to Hum. 97 Trumpet Boy.

PLQF-98A, similar to Hum. 98 Sister.

Music Boxes, Revolving Musical Figurines

This section introduces two music boxes and the revolving musical figurines that range from Hummel-inspired to "stretch" Hummel designs at best. The items shown should also be considered a form of Hummel hybrid as previously discussed in the Planters introduction and have no Hummel parallels as musicals.

The music boxes speak for themselves (no pun intended). The revolving musical figurines demand further discussion, particularly those by Willitts Designs of Petaluma, California. Willitts marketed an interesting half dozen, better-quality revolving musical figurines equipped with the highly respected Sankyo Musical Movements. This entire six-piece group was offered for sale in the Willitts Designs 1985 product catalog, but all have since been discontinued.

Ignoring the Willitts' musical features and comparing only their individual figurine designs with that of Goebel's Hummel figurines, you will see a very close similarity manifested in three pieces in particular. Remove the goose from RMF-7A (Willitts' Item No. 8740) and you have a very good copy of Goebel's Hum. 7 Merry Wanderer, including the raised index finger of his right hand. Remove the West Highland white terrier from RMF-135A (Willitts' Item No. 8742) and you will find Goebel's Hum.

135 Soloist. Make a couple of minor adjustments to RMF-136A (Willitts' Item No. 8745) and you have Goebel's Hum. 136 Friends. The most stretchy comparison would be RMF-15A (Willitts' Item No. 8741), which reminds one of a "Hear Ye, Hear Ye" in a "Just Resting" position. You can see that it does retain many of the "Hear Ye, Hear Ye" elements. For a final stretchy, consider exchanging the rocking horse on RMF-17A (Willitts' Item No. 8744) for the planter with bird of Goebel's Hum. 17, and what do you have? Right—"Congratulations!"

Cook Brothers, of Chicago, Illinois, offered two very good revolving musical figurine copycats of Goebel's Hum. 218 Birthday Serenade and Hum. 336 Close Harmony in their 1984-85 Wholesale Catalog. The two are Cook Brothers Item No. 2927B and 2927A, shown in the following pages as RFM-218A and RMF-336A. No additives or take-aways necessary in these two comparisons.

I have been known to overreact in these areas and tend to stretch the stretch Hummels at times. I ask myself, "Could Humpty Dumpty possibly be a stretch Hummel?" (That is a little self-test I use now and then to check my rationale.) My answer is—usually—never!

Hum. 7/0 Merry Wanderer, TMK-3.

RMF-7A, USA, 7″ high. Note the addition of goose companion.

140

MBX-57A music box has POP plaque inset similar to "Chick Girl" in bas-relief. Wall mounted. Pull cord to play. Melody: "Chim Chim Cher-ee."

MBX-58A music box has a POP plaque inset similar to "Playmates" in bas-relief. Wall mounted. Pull cord to play. Melody: "Talk to the Animals."

RMF-7A is shown on page 47 of Willitts Designs 1985 Catalog as Item No. 8740. The figurine is similar to Goebel's Hum. 7 Merry Wanderer. Melody: "Singin' in the Rain." RMF-15A is shown on page 47 of Willitts Designs 1985 Catalog as Item No. 8741. The figurine was possibly inspired by Goebel's Hum. 15 Hear Ye, Hear Ye. Melody: "Edelweiss."

See pages 142-44 for photographs of the following: RMF-17A is shown on page 47 of Willitts Designs 1985 Catalog as Item No. 8744. The figurine was possibly inspired by Goebel's Hum. 17 Congratulations. Melody: "Toyland."

RMF-47A is shown on page 47 of Willitts Designs 1985 Catalog as Item No. 8743. The figurine was possibly inspired by Goebel's Hum. 47 Goose Girl. Melody: "Fur Elise."

RMF-135A is shown on page 47 of Willitts Designs 1985 Catalog as Item No. 8742. The figurine is similar to Goebel's Hum. 135 Soloist. Melody: "I'd Like to Teach the World to Sing." RMF-136A is shown on page 47 of Willitts Designs 1985 Catalog as Item No. 8745. The figurine is similar to Goebel's Hum. 136 Friends. Melody: "It's a Small World."

Hum. 57/1 Chick Girl, TMK-6.

Hum. 58/0 Playmates, TMK-6.

MBX-57A, Japan, wooden, 6⅝"h × 5⅝" w × 3"d.

MBX-58A, Japan, wooden, 6¾"h × 5⅝" w × 2¾"d.

Music Boxes, etc. (continued)

Hum. 15/0 Hear ye, Hear ye, TMK-5.

RMF-15A, USA, 6¾" high. Truly a stretch Hummel look-alike. I call it a "Just Resting Hear Ye, Hear Ye."

Hum. 17/0 Congratulations, with socks, TMK-6.

RMF-17A, USA, 7". Planter with bird replaced by a rocking horse.

Hum. 47/0 Goose Girl, TMK-5.

RMF-47A, USA, 7″. One goose must have waddled off somewhere.

Hum. 94/I Surprise, TMK-6.

RMF-94A, Taiwan, bisque, 7⅜″, melody, "Edelweiss."

143

RMF-94B, Taiwan, bisque, 7⅛″, melody, "Edelweiss."

RMF-135A, USA, 6⅞″. Note the addition of a West Highland white terrier.

Hum. 135 Soloist, TMK-5.

Hum. 136/I Friends, TMK-6.

RMF-136A, USA, 6¾″.

Music Boxes, etc. (continued)

RMF-218A is shown on page 29 of Cook Bros. 1984-85 Wholesale Catalog as Item No. 2927B. The figurine is similar to Goebel's Hum. 218 Birthday Serenade. Melody: "Lorelei." RMF-336A is shown on page 29 of Cook Bros. 1984-85 Wholesale Catalog as Item No. 2927A. The figurine is similar to Goebel's Hum. 336 Close Harmony. Melody: "Edelweiss."

Hum. 218/2/0 Birthday Serenade, TMK-4.

RMF-218A, Taiwan, bisque, 6⅝". Large tree stump added behind children.

Hum. 336 Close Harmony, TMK-6.

RMF-336A, Taiwan, bisque, 7".

Table Lamps

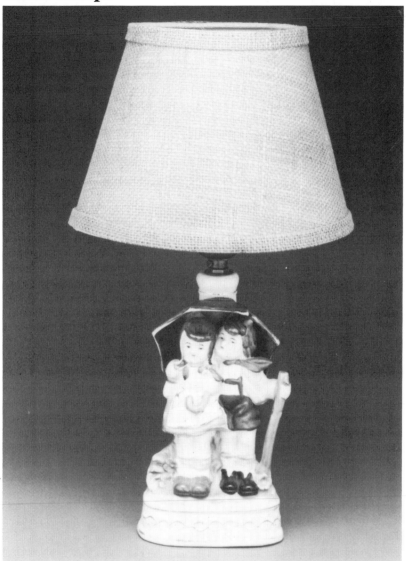

TLP-71A, a unique Hummel-inspired Stormy Weather table lamp has no Goebel Hummel counterpart. Marked "Made in Occupied Japan" (r), 7¾" h × 4½" w base. Overall height including shade is 15". A rare find. See TLP-47A Goose Girl table lamp.

Key to Symbols

Hummel Copycat code: HC—Hummel copycat; HCM—mini-size; BE—bookend; BVS—bud vase; CDL—candleholder; MBX—music box; MC—Mel copycat; PLQ—plaque; PLQF—plaque figurine; PTR—planter; REL—religious message figurine; RMF—revolving musical figurine; SPS—salt and pepper shakers; TLP—table lamp; TPK—toothpick holder; WVS—wall vase. *Note:* Unless otherwise specified, all copycats pictured are made of ceramic.

Alphabetical Guide and Values for Hummel Copycats

(Key to Symbols, opposite.)

Hummel Name	Copycat No.	Size	Origin	Type	Value
Adoration	HC-23A	6½"	Japan	F	$ 35
	HC-23B	8¾"	USA(?)	F	NQV
Adoration w/Bird	HC-105A	4⅜"	Japan(?)	F	27
Angel, Joyous News w/Lute, Candleholder	CDL-38A	2⅞"	MIOJ	CDL	15
Angel, Joyous News w/Accordion, Candleholder	CDL-39A	2¾"	MIOJ	CDL	15
Angel, Joyous News w/Trumpet, Candleholder	CDL-40A	2⅞"	MIOJ	CDL	15
Angel Serenade	HC-83A	5¾"	Japan(?)	F	35
Angel Trio (B) (Set)	HC-238/AA	2¼"	Japan(?)	F	3
	HC-238/AB	2⅛"	MIOJ	F	8
	HC-238/AC	2¼"	Japan(?)	F	3
	HC-238/BA	2"	Japan(?)	F	3
	HC-238/BB	2⅛"	MIOJ	F	8
	HC-238/BC	2"	Japan(?)	F	3
	HC-238/CA	2¼"	Japan(?)	F	3
	HC-238/CB	2⅛"	MIOJ	F	8
	HC-238/CC	2¼"	Japan(?)	F	3
	SPS-238/AA	2¼"	Japan	SPS	3
	SPS-238/CA	2"	Japan	SPS	3
Angelic Sleep, w/Candleholder	HC-25A	3⅛"	MIOJ	F	38
	HC-25B	4⅛"	MIOJ	F	55
Apple Tree Boy	HC-142A	6¼"	Japan	F	27
	HC-142B	6⅛"	Japan	F	25
	HC-142C	4⅛"	Hong Kong	F	2
Apple Tree Girl	HC-141A	6¼"	Japan(?)	F	25
	HC-141B	4⅛"	Hong Kong	F	2
	HC-141C	4¼"	Hong Kong	F	2
Baker	HC-128A	5¼"	Japan	F	22
Band Leader	HC-129A	6"	Japan(?)	F	17
Barnyard Hero	HC-195A	5"	Taiwan	F	15
Be Patient	HC-197A	4¼"	Hong Kong	F	2
Birthday Serenade	RMF-218A	6⅝"	Taiwan	RMF	22
Book Worm	HC-8A	4"	USA	F	15
Book Worm, Bookends	BE-14/AA	4"	USA	BE	15
	BE-14/AB	5½"	MIOJ	BE	38
	BE-14/AC	6"	Japan(?)	BE	13
	BE-14/AD	5¼"	Japan	BE	15

Hummel Name	Copycat No.	Size	Origin	Type	Value
	BE-14/BA	4″	USA	BE	$15
	BE-14/BB	5⅝″	MIOJ	BE	38
	PTR-14/BA	5⅝″	Japan(?)	PTR	10
Boots	HC-143A	5⅝″	Japan	F	22
	HC-143B	6″	Japan	F	26
	HCM-143A	3″	Japan(?)	F	15
Boy w/Horse	HC-239/CA	3⅛″	MIOJ	F	8
	HC-239/CB	3⅛″	Japan	F	3
	PTR-239/CA	3¼″	MIOJ	PTR	9
	SPS-239/CA	4½″	Japan	SPS	4
	SPS-239/CB	4⅜″	MIOJ	SPS	8
	SPS-239/CC	4⅜″	MIOJ	SPS	8
Boy w/Toothache	HC-217A	5½″	OJ	F	65
	HCM-217A	3¼″	Japan(?)	F	15
Brother	HC-95A	5½″	USA(?)	F	13
	HC-95B	4¾″	Unknown	F	10
	HC-95C	5½″	USA	F	10
	BE-95A	4¾″	USA(?)	BE	37
	PLQF-95A	4⅜″	USA(?)	PLQF	6
	REL-95A	5¾″	USA(?)	F	32
Chick Girl	HC-57A	4″	Japan	F	35
	HC-57B	4⅜″	USA(?)	F	17
	HC-57C	4⅜″	USA	F	35
	HC-57D	3¾″	Unknown	F	10
	HC-57E	4″	MIOJ	F	18
	MBX-57A	6⅝″	Japan	MBX	17
	PTR-57A	4½″	Japan	PTR	12
Chick Girl, Bookend	BE-61/BA	4⅜″	Spain	BE	48
Children Trio (A) Set	HC-239/AA	3⅛″	Japan	F	3
	HC-239/BA	3⅛″	MIOJ	F	8
	HC-239/CA	3⅛″	MIOJ	F	8
	HC-239/CB	3⅛″	Japan	F	3
	SPS-239/AA	4⅜″	MIOJ	SPS	8
	SPS-239/AB	4¼″	MIOJ	SPS	8
	SPS-239/AC	4⅜″	MIOJ	SPS	8
	SPS-239/BA	4¼″	Japan	SPS	4
	SPS-239/BB	4¼″	MIOJ	SPS	8
	SPS-239/CA	4½″	Japan	SPS	4
	SPS-239/CB	4⅜″	MIOJ	SPS	8
	SPS-239/CC	4⅜″	MIOJ	SPS	8
Close Harmony	RMF-336A	7″	Taiwan	RMF	22
Confidentially	HC-314A	5½″	OJ	F	18
Congratulations	HC-17A	5¾″	USA(?)	F	25
	RMF-17A	7″	USA	RMF	45
Culprits	HC-56/AA	6¼″	USA	F	42
	HC-56/AB	6⅝″	Taiwan	F	15
Doctor	HC-127A	5″	OJ	F	65
	HC-127B	4⅞″	Japan	F	16
	HC-127C	4¼″	Japan(?)	F	13
	HC-127D	4⅞″	MIOJ	F	35
	HC-127E	5¾″	MIOJ	F	45
	HC-127F	5⅜″	Japan(?)	F	10
Doll Mother	HC-67A	4⅝″	MIOJ	F	65

Hummel Name	Copycat No.	Size	Origin	Type	Value
	HC-67B	4⅜″	USA	F	$ 22
	HC-67C	4¾″	Japan(?)	F	13
	HC-67D	4½″	USA(?)	F	17
	PTR-67A	3½″	Japan	PTR	8
	PTR-67B	4⅞″	Japan(?)	PTR	11
	TPK-67A	4½″	MIOJ	TPK	18
Duet	HC-130A	11⅛″	Japan(?)	F	NQV
	HC-130B	5¼″	Japan(?)	F	20
Eventide	HC-99A	4″	Japan(?)	F	10
	HC-99B	3⅞″	MIOJ	F	15
	HC-99C	4¼″	Japan	F	12
Farewell	HC-65A	4½″	USA(?)	F	15
	HC-65B	4½″	MIOJ	F	13
	HC-65C	5⅝″	MIOJ	F	15
	PTR-65A	3⅛″	Japan	PTR	12
	REL-65A	4½″	USA(?)	F	32
Farm Boy	HC-66A	5¼″	Taiwan	F	15
	HC-66B	5″	USA	F	13
	HC-66C	5″	USA	F	17
Farm Boy, Bookend	BE-60/AA	4½″	Spain	BE	48
Feathered Friends	HC-344A	4⅝″	Taiwan	F	15
Flower Madonna	HC-10A	8⅝″	USA(?)	F	NQV
Forest Shrine	HC-183A	6″	Japan(?)	F	27
For Father	HC-87A	5⅜″	Japan	F	15
Friends	RMF-136A	6¾″	USA	RMF	45
Girl w/Doll	HC-239/BA	3⅛″	MIOJ	F	8
	SPS-239/BA	4¼″	Japan	SPS	4
	SPS-239/BB	4¼″	MIOJ	SPS	8
Girl w/Nosegay	HC-239/AA	3⅛″	Japan	F	3
	SPS-239/AA	4⅜″	MIOJ	SPS	8
	SPS-239/AB	4¼″	MIOJ	SPS	8
	SPS-239/AC	4⅜″	MIOJ	SPS	8
Globe Trotter	HC-79A	3¾″	Japan	F	10
	HC-79B	5″	USA	F	15
	HC-79C	4⅞″	Japan	F	12
	HC-79D	5⅞″	MIOJ	F	23
	HC-79E	6¾″	Taiwan	F	15
Going to Grandma's	HC-52A	4⅜″	Unknown	F	45
Good Friends	HC-182A	4″	Spain	F	35
Good Friends, Bookend	BE-251/AA	3¾″	Spain	BE	42
Good Hunting	PTR-307A	3″	Japan	PTR	4
Good Shepherd	HC-42A	6⅛″	USA(?)	F	25
Goose Girl	HC-47A	5¼″	MIOJ	F	125
	HC-47B	3⅞″	Hong Kong	F	2
	HC-47C	4½″	MIOJ	F	38
	HC-47D	4¾″	USA	F	22
	HC-47E	5″	Japan	F	15
	HC-47F	5⅜″	USA(?)	F	15
	HC-47G	5″	Japan	F	27
	HC-47H	5⅝″	Japan(?)	F	15
	HC-47J	7⅜″	USA(?)	F	13
	HCM-47A	3″	USA	F	15
	BVS-47A	5⅛″	Japan	BVS	6

Hummel Name	Copycat No.	Size	Origin	Type	Value
	PTR-47A	3″	Japan(?)	PTR	$ 4
	PTR-47B	5¾″	Japan	PTR	8
	RMF-47A	7″	USA	RMF	45
	TLP-47A	7¾″	USA(?)	TLP	25
Goose Girl, Bookend	BE-60/BA	4¼″	Spain	BE	48
Happiness	HC-86A	5¼″	Japan	F	22
	HC-86B	4¼″	USA(?)	F	13
	HC-86C	4″	Japan	F	10
	HC-86D	4⅜″	Hong Kong	F	2
	HC-86E	4″	MIOJ	F	13
	WVS-86A	5¼″	Japan	WVS	12
Happy Birthday	HC-176A	5⅛″	Japan(?)	F	32
Happy Pastime	HC-69A	3¾″	MIOJ	F	28
	HC-69B	3½″	USA	F	15
	HC-69C	3⅞″	USA	F	15
	HC-69D	2¾″	Japan	F	10
	HC-69E	3″	USA(?)	F	15
	PTR-69A	4″	Japan	PTR	12
Happy Traveller	HC-109A	5½″	Japan(?)	F	12
Hear Ye, Hear Ye	HC-15A	5⅜″	USA	F	17
	HC-15B	5⅝″	USA(?)	F	17
	HC-15C	5⅝″	USA	F	25
	HC-15D	4⅜″	Japan(?)	F	10
	HC-15E	5⅜″	Japan	F	15
	RMF-15A	6¾″	USA	RMF	45
Heavenly Angel	HC-21A	4¼″	USA(?)	F	17
Heavenly Song, Candleholder	CDL-113A	3⅜″	Unknown	CDL	75
Hello	HC-124A	5⅝″	Hong Kong	F	3
Joyful	HC-53A	3¼″	USA(?)	F	15
	HC-53B	4⅛″	Japan	F	13
	HC-53C	3⅞″	MIOJ	F	28
Just Resting	HC-112A	5″	USA	F	18
	PTR-112A	4⅜″	Japan	PTR	9
Latest News	HC-184A	5″	Japan	F	35
	HC-184B	3⅞″	Japan	F	10
	HC-184C	5¼″	Japan	F	45
Let's Sing	HC-110A	4⅛″	USA(?)	F	13
Little Cellist	HC-89A	5¾″	USA	F	16
	HC-89B	4½″	Japan	F	10
	HC-89C	7½″	USA(?)	F	13
	HC-89D	4⅝″	MIOJ	F	18
Little Fiddler	HC-2A	4⅜″	MIOJ	F	13
	HC-2B	4⅞″	MIOJ	F	18
	HC-2C	4½″	MIOJ	F	13
	HC-2D	7¾″	USA	F	22
	SPS-2A	4⅜″	MIOJ	SPS	10
	HC-4A	5″	USA(?)	F	15
	HC-4B	5″	Unknown	F	10
Little Gardner	HC-74A	5½″	Japan	F	22
Little Hiker	HC-16A	5⅛″	Taiwan	F	15
	HC-16B	4″	Japan	F	7
	HC-16C	4¼″	Japan	F	7
	HC-16D	5⅛″	USA	F	15

Hummel Name	Copycat No.	Size	Origin	Type	Value
	HC-16E	5″	Unknown	F	$10
	HC-16F	5½″	USA(?)	F	15
	HC-16G	5⅛″	Japan(?)	F	22
	HC-16H	5⅜″	MIOJ	F	28
	BE-16A	6″	Japan	BE	15
	SPS-16A	4⅜″	MIOJ	SPS	8
Little Shopper	HC-96A	4¾″	Japan	F	10
	PLQ-96A	8″	USA(?)	PLQ	35
	PLQF-96A	3¾″	USA(?)	PLQF	6
	PTR-96A	4″	MIOJ	PTR	13
Lost Sheep	HC-68A	4⅞″	MIOJ	F	35
	REL-68A	5⅜″	USA(?)	F	32
March Winds	HC-43A	4⅞″	USA(?)	F	15
	HC-43B	4¾″	Japan	F	7
Meditation	HC-13A	5″	Japan	F	13
	HC-13B	5¼″	OJ	F	65
	HC-13C	5″	Japan(?)	F	7
	HC-13D	5⅜″	USA(?)	F	18
	PTR-13A	5⅛″	MIOJ	PTR	15
Merry Wanderer	HC-7A	5¾″	Hong Kong	F	15
	HC-7B	5½″	USA	F	25
	HC-7C	5″	Unknown	F	15
	HC-7D	4⅝″	Japan	F	7
	HC-7E	6⅞″	Taiwan	F	15
	RMF-7A	7″	USA	RMF	45
Mischief Maker	HC-342A	4⅞″	Taiwan	F	15
Not for You	HC-317A	5¼″	MIOJ	F	14
Out of Danger	HC-56/BA	6¾″	Taiwan	F	15
Playmates	HC-58A	4⅛″	Japan	F	35
	HC-58B	4⅜″	USA(?)	F	15
	HC-58C	4½″	USA	F	18
	HC-58D	4⅜″	USA	F	15
	MBX-58A	6¾″	Japan	MBX	17
Playmates, Bookend	BE-61/AA	4⅝″	Spain	BE	48
Postman	HC-119A	5⅝″	MIOJ	F	35
	HC-119B	5⅜″	Japan	F	7
	HC-119C	5⅞″	Japan(?)	F	15
	PTR-119A	4″	Japan(?)	PTR	45
Prayer Before Battle	HC-20A	4¼″	USA(?)	F	22
	HC-20B	4¾″	OJ	F	65
	PTR-20A	2⅞″	MIOJ	PTR	9
Puppy Love	HC-1A	5″	USA	F	20
	HC-1B	4¾″	MIOJ	F	18
	HC-1C	5⅜″	Japan	F	13
	HC-1D	4¼″	MIOJ	F	15
	HC-1E	5⅛″	MIOJ	F	23
	PTR-1A	2¾″	MIOJ	PTR	9
	PTR-1B	3¼″	Japan	PTR	10
	PTR-1C	2⅞″	Japan	PTR	4
	PTR-1D	5¼″	Japan	PTR	8
	PTR-1E	5¼″	Japan	PTR	8
Retreat to Safety	HC-201A	3¾″	Hong Kong	F	3
	HC-201B	4⅞″	USA	F	25

Hummel Name	Copycat No.	Size	Origin	Type	Value
School Boy	HC-82A	5″	USA	F	$17
	HC-82B	5⅛″	USA(?)	F	15
	HC-82C	5⅝″	OJ	F	65
	HC-82D	4¾″	Unknown	F	10
	BVS-82A	5″	USA	BVS	20
	PLQF-82A	4¼″	USA(?)	PLQF	6
School Girl	HC-81A	5″	USA	F	15
	BVS-81A	5⅛″	USA	BVS	20
	PLQF-81A	4⅜″	USA(?)	PLQF	6
	REL-81A	5⅛″	USA(?)	F	32
Serenade	HC-85A	5¾″	MIOJ	F	35
	HC-85B	5⅝″	Hong Kong	F	3
	HC-85C	5⅜″	Japan	F	10
	HC-85D	5″	Japan(?)	F	10
	HC-85E	4⅝″	USA	F	12
	HC-85F	4⅜″	MIOJ	F	13
She Loves Me, She Loves Me Not	HC-174A	4″	Spain	F	35
She loves Me, She Loves Me Not, Bookend	BE-251/BA	4″	Spain	BE	42
Shepherd's Boy	HC-64A	5⅝″	USA(?)	F	17
Silent Night, Candleholder	CDL-54A	4″	Japan(?)	CDL	45
Singing Lesson	HC-63A	3″	Japan	F	12
	HC-63B	3″	MIOJ	F	17
	HC-63C	2¾″	USA(?)	F	15
	PTR-63A	3½″	MIOJ	PTR	13
	PTR-63B	2⅞″	Japan	PTR	4
	WVS-63A	5¼″	Japan	WVS	12
Sister	HC-98A	5⅜″	USA(?)	F	15
	HC-98B	5⅝″	MIOJ	F	45
	HC-98C	5¼″	MIOJ	F	35
	HC-98D	5″	Japan(?)	F	7
	HC-98E	5½″	Japan(?)	F	10
	HC-97/98A	5⅜″	USA(?)	F	25
	BE-98A	5″	USA(?)	BE	37
	PLQF-98A	4⅜″	USA(?)	PLQF	6
Skier	HC-59A	5¼″	USA(?)	F	125
Soloist	HC-135A	3⅞″	Japan(?)	F	7
	HC-135B	5″	Japan	F	10
	RMF-135A	6⅞″	USA	RMF	45
Star Gazer	HC-132A	4¼″	OJ	F	65
	HC-132B	3⅞″	Japan(?)	F	12
	HC-132C	4⅜″	Japan(?)	F	17
	HCM-132A	2½″	Japan(?)	F	15
Stormy Weather	HC-71A	5⅝″	Japan(?)	F	15
	HC-71B	6¼″	USA(?)	F	18
	HC-71C	5⅞″	MIOJ	F	45
	HC-71D	6½″	USA	F	30
	TLP-71A	7¾″	MIOJ	TLP	85
Street Singer	HC-131A	5″	Hong Kong	F	2
	HC-131B	5½″	Japan	F	12
Strolling Along	HC-5A	5⅞″	USA(?)	F	17

Hummel Name	Copycat No.	Size	Origin	Type	Value
	HC-5B	6⅝″	Taiwan	F	$15
	HC-5C	5″	OJ	F	28
	REL-5A	4⅞″	USA(?)	F	32
Surprise	HC-94A	5⅛″	USA(?)	F	15
	HC-94B	1½″	Hong Kong	F	7
	HC-94C	4⅞″	Japan	F	12
	RMF-94A	7⅜″	Taiwan	RMF	22
	RMF-94B	7⅛″	Taiwan	RMF	22
To Market	HC-49A	4¾″	Japan	F	15
	HC-49B	4½″	MIOJ	F	23
	HC-49C	5⅛″	Japan	F	15
	HC-49D	5⅜″	MIOJ	F	38
	HC-49E	5⅛″	Japan(?)	F	15
	HC-49F	5⅜″	USA	F	20
Trumpet Boy	HC-97A	5⅛″	USA(?)	F	12
	HC-97B	4¾″	Unknown	F	10
	HC-97/98A	5⅜″	USA(?)	F	25
	PLQF-97A	4⅛″	USA(?)	PLQF	6
Umbrella Boy	HC-152/AA	5″	Spain	F	60
	BE-152/AA	5″	Spain	BE	72
Umbrella Girl	HC-152/BA	4⅞″	Spain	F	60
	BE-152/BA	4⅞″	Spain	BE	72
Village Boy	HC-51A	4½″	Hong Kong	F	2
	TPK-51A	4⅜″	MIOJ	TPK	18
Volunteers	HC-50A	5⅛″	Japan	F	16
	HC-50B	5¼″	MIOJ	F	38
	HC-50C	6¼″	Japan	F	22
	HC-50D	5⅝″	Japan(?)	F	22
Wash Day	HC-321A	5⅝″	Japan(?)	F	15
Watchful Angel	HC-194A	5¾″	Japan	F	45
Wayside Devotion	HC-28A	7¼″	USA(?)	F	135
Wayside Harmony	HC-111A	5⅞″	Taiwan	F	10
Worship	HC-84A	5½″	Japan(?)	F	22

Mel Name	Copycat No.	Size	Origin	Type	Value
Child in Bed	MC-6A	4⅛″	OJ	CBX	125

Occupied Japan

Those Topsy-Turvy Hummel Copycats

Once upon a time not too long ago, the Japanese were renowned as the copycat masters of the world. But today, in a historic reversal, the world is trying to copy the Japanese. This section relates to the "not too long ago" era and the upside-down world of the Occupied Japan Hummel copycat collector.

The title "Topsy-Turvy" and/or upside-down world is quite appropriate. In fact it would also be a fitting caption for collectors of genuine Goebel Hummel figurines. The OJ collector turns the figurine upside-down to see if it possesses the "Made in Occupied Japan" or "Occupied Japan" mark. The Goebel Hummel collector, doing likewise, is checking for one of the several Hummel trademarks, Crown, Full Bee, Stylized Bee, to name a few. It would be great if these types of collectibles were made with flat heads. Then we could display them with bases up and would never have to turn them over again.

I developed an affection for Japan while on an eighteen-month tour of duty (1954-1955) as a member of the United States Air Force, stationed at Tokyo International Airport, Haneda, Japan. During this period I gained an above-average knowledge of Japanese collectibles, whether they be arms and armor, powder flasks, or MIOJ Hummel look-alikes, which has added collecting depth, understanding, and appreciation to my current propensity, the collecting of "Occupied Japan" Hummel copycats.

The OJ figurines are intermingled throughout the book in numerical sequence according to their Goebel Hummel counterpart, with sizes, marks, color of marks, and pertinent comments, if any. All the Occupied Japan figurines were then assembled for a family portrait and are shown in several color photographs. Each is identified by its Hummel counterpart's number. For more detailed information in regard to any figurine in the color photographs, refer to the Index to locate the black and white photograph.

The abbreviations MIOJ (Made in Occupied Japan) and OJ (Occupied Japan) are used in the photograph captions to indicate how the figurine is actually marked. Color of the mark is symbolized by a lower case letter, in parentheses: (b) black; (g) green; and (r) red; because some collectors of OJ are interested in the ink color used.

Markings of Articles for Export

Occupied Japan collectibles are marked in one of two ways: "Made in Occupied Japan" or "Occupied Japan." The period of the American Occupation of Japan after World War II extended from September 2, 1945, to April 28, 1952, when the Occupation officially ended. But that is not the time frame in which the Japanese products marked "Made in Occupied Japan" or "Occupied Japan" were actually required to be marked as such. Bob W. Gee, president of the Occupied Japan Collectors Club and editor of its newsletter, revealed in Volume 1, Number 8, published August 1982, a copy of SCAPIN 1535 (Supreme Commander for the Allied Powers Instructions) dated 20 February 1947, which was a memorandum to the Imperial Japanese Government reading as follows:

Subject: Marking of Export Articles

1. The Imperial Japanese Government is hereby directed to take immediate steps to insure that every article prepared for export after 15 days of receipt of this Directive, the immediate container thereof and the outside package will be marked, stamped, branded or labeled in legible English with the words "Made in Occupied Japan."

2. All marking, stamping, branding or labeling shall be made in a conspicuous place and shall be as nearly indelible and permanent as the nature of the article will permit.

Assuming those concerned received that directive immediately, then the earliest required date for the marking "Made in Occupied Japan" would have been March 7, 1947.

The aforementioned SCAPIN 1535 was rescinded and made optional in SCAPIN 2061, dated 5 December 1949. The general consensus is that the majority of the

Sampling of "Made in Occupied Japan" and "Occupied Japan" Marks and Base Designs

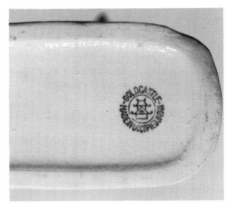

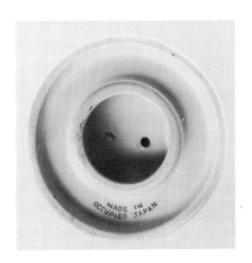

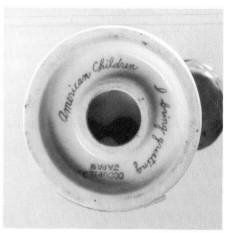

Japanese manufacturers continued with the mark "Made in Occupied Japan" or just "Occupied Japan" until April 28, 1952, the end of the American Occupation, which would encompass an approximate five-year marking span.

There are other rulings on record that indicate that the Japanese products could be marked either "Made in Occupied Japan," "Occupied Japan," "Made in Japan," or "Japan." Again, the consensus is that the latter two marks, "Made in Japan" or "Japan," were rarely used, if not discarded altogether, during the remaining forty-two months or so of the Occupation. Reasoning being that the Japanese merchants did not want to risk rejection of their goods for improper origin marking, and almost faithfully used the "Made in Occupied Japan" or "Occupied Japan" marks. They may have also felt that the inclusion of the designation "Occupied" on their products would make them less objectionable to the American consumer.

American Children Hummel Copycats

Worthy of further comment are those very good look-alikes, "American Children." This particular series has become very popular and most sought after within the ranks of Occupied Japan collectors in addition to being pursued by Hummel copycat fanciers and the occasional Goebel Hummel collector. The American Children figurines are of good quality but not up to Goebel's high standards.

Upon first acquiring these figurines, I was convinced that all those marked "American Children" were copies of Goebel's Hummels, until I purchased one marked "Concert" of a lederhosen-clad boy standing and accompanying a singing frog on his mandolin. I have not located any Hummel parallel for this piece and have since heard of other non-Hummel American Children pieces. Further, not all American Children figurines are marked "Made in Occupied Japan" or Occupied Japan." I have two non-Occupied American Children Hummel copycats, HC-128A and HC-184C, both with a "Leftons Exclusives Japan" foil label. This leads me to believe that both Occupied and non-Occupied American Children figurines were distributed by Leftons Exclusives out of Chicago, Illinois.

A unique American Children figurine is the scarce copycat of Goebel's Mel 6 candy box, "Child in Bed," shown in black and white in this section as MC-6, and also included in the Color Section. This excellent, mint condition piece was acquired from a dealer in Royal Oak, Michigan, about three years ago for twenty-two dollars. Marked in two lines (red cursive) "American Children—Cradle Boy," with a two-line (black letters) "Occupied Japan," I consider it one of my prime copycats. Indications are that Goebel's Mel 6 figurine was designed from a Sister Hummel drawing but was either never approved or never submitted to the Franciscan Convent for approval by Goebel. Consequently, this Mel figurine was never assigned a Hummel series number, nor was it to be incised with the M. I. Hummel signature. The Goebel Company elected to use the derivative Mel, the last three letters of the Hummel name, to indicate it was, indeed, a member of the Hummel family.

Several other American Children figurines are known that are now in private collections. Possibly, when a revised edition of this book is published, we will be able to include them along with additional Hummel copycats with Occupied Japan origins.

Child in Bed, Mel. 6
("Baby in a Basket," "Box with Child in Bed on Top")

Mel 6, Child in Bed, candy box. Discontinued by Goebel in 1962. Rue Dee Marker collection.

MC-6A, markings bottom of candy box.

MC-6A, candy box, top and bottom.

MC-6A, candy box, OJ(b), "American Children—Cradle Boy"(r), 4⅛" h × 3¼" w × 4⅝" l. A unique Hummel copycat.

Occupied Japan Collectors Clubs

Recommended clubs: Two principal clubs I can recommend from personal experience as I am a member of both organizations are:

Occupied Japan Collectors Club
18309 Faysmith Avenue
Torrance, California 90504
Club President and Editor: Bob W. Gee
Publication: Quarterly Newsletter
Annual Membership Dues: $6.50

The O.J. Club
c/o Florence Archambault
29 Freeborn Street
Newport, Rhode Island 02840
Club President and Editor: Florence Archambault
Publication: Monthly newsletter titled
"The Upside Down World of an O.J. Collector"
Annual Membership Dues: $10.00

Herbert Dubler Figurines

L ove those Dubler kids from New York! What a great bunch of talented guys and dolls. You'll find the brassy "Boy with Tuba," a swinging saxophonist, an ever-so-vibrant "Boy with Drum," and a sweet 'n' easy flautist, all harmoniously directed by their vigorous "Band Leader." What more can one ask for musically, except possibly to be captivated by the New Orleans style jazz sounds of the "Little Bugler" who hasn't joined my combo yet. I have been searching for this missing Dubler musician for quite some time. Heard he was doing a gig somewhere in Manhattan. Find that boy and it's "hello" Carnegie Hall!

The New Orleans style Dubler jazz combo.

Let's not forget some of the other gifted Dubler children, like "Little Mother," "Little Mailman," and "Little Cobbler," who always appear to be singing their hearts out. Sort of a "great to be alive" trio. One look at "Doll's Doctor" and you immediately share his concern. How about the "Little Chemist" who seems convinced he has discovered the cure for the common cold. Is the "Little Bookworm" truly reciting Shakespeare? And finally, but not finally, a totally exhausted "Sleepy Baby" enjoying his half-price ticket to an off-off Broadway show.

Admittedly appealing, these "American Hummels" possess a tangled background that has intrigued collectors for years. The consensus is that the firm of Herbert Dubler, Inc. began copyrighting and producing Hummel figurines, cards, and prints during World War II to take advantage of the export gap created when wartime embargoes restricted the importing into the U.S. of any goods originating from Germany. The validity of international copyright protection was tested and possibly infringed upon, if not totally disregarded, during this wartime period. Whether or not it was legal is unclear, but Herbert Dubler, Inc. did, indeed, register copyrights for Hummel cards, prints, and Hummel figurines.

Furthermore, the House of Ars Sacra, Herbert Dubler, Inc. also maintained in

The "Great to be Alive" Dubler trio!

159

The charming little figurines shown on the following pages have been created by Ars Sacra and are authentic reproductions of the original designs by Berta Hummel and other well-known artists. They are made of a plaster composition and are artistically hand-decorated in our own studio. Thus, some of the most appealing greeting card designs by Berta Hummel and other artists that have captivated thousands of people all over the country have now come to life in the form of these fine little figurines.

THEY ARE PRICED AS FOLLOWS:

No. 33—The Tiny Cherub, by E. O. Jones   @ $2.00 each retail
No. 31—The Little Skipper, by E. O. Jones @ $2.50 each retail
All Other Figures, by B. Hummel   @ $3.00 each retail

Usual Trade Discount

THE HOUSE OF ARS SACRA

HERBERT DUBLER, Inc.
251 FOURTH AVENUE, NEW YORK, N. Y.

The House of Ars Sacra, Herbert Dubler, Inc. brochure, page 1. (C. 1942)

No. 39—The Sleepy Baby   No. 33—The Tiny Cherub   No. 41—Hello! Birdie

No. 35—The Little Mailman   No. 31—The Little Skipper   No. 36—The Little Cobbler

Brochure, page 2. (C. 1942).

their advertising brochure that "A royalty from the sale of the figures will go to the artist that designed them. In the case of Berta Hummel, the royalty will be paid to a trust in her name, to be distributed among the Franciscan Convents in this country at her own discretion. . . ." It has never been documented that actual distribution of these royalties ever took place.

Documented Corporate History

Herbert Dubler, Inc. produced authentic Hummel figurines during the 1940s. At the time of incorporation, filed April 20, 1939, their business address was listed at 15 Barclay Street, New York, New York, retaining the address of the firm then owned by Herbert Dubler, an importer of greeting cards, prints, and other paper products. The firm later moved to 251 Fourth Avenue, New York 10, New York. It is reported that Herbert Dubler, also referred to as Dr. Herbert Dubler, was a Swiss citizen with a doctorate in canon law. He was known to be a relative of the family that controlled Verlag Ars Sacra, Joseph Müller in Munich, the company that was the first to publish Hummel graphics. He returned to Germany some time following the sale of Herbert Dubler, Inc. to Messrs. John P. McArdle, Herman T. VanMell, and Lawrence B. Wardrop, Jr., residents of the New York area. According to their Certificate of Incorporation, the purpose for which it was formed was to purchase and continue the business owned by Herbert Dubler and . . .

> To manufacture, print, publish, circulate, distribute, import, export, buy, sell and deal in books, pamphlets, magazines, newspapers, pictures, cards, music and anything which may be printed, engraved, lithographed or electrotyped; to acquire by purchase or otherwise, license the use of, assign and deal with, copyrights and intellectual properties of every kind.

Since there was no direct mention of the new corporation buying or distributing figurines, it would appear that figurines, and particularly Hummel-type figurine adaptations, were not then being considered as a part of their product line. They were, however, producing and distributing Hummel greeting cards, note cards, and prints. It is unknown to me how the figurine product line evolved within the Herbert

Dubler Corporation. Through my research I have determined that Joseph Josephu, a gifted, professional sculptor, played a major roll in the development of the Dubler Hummel line of figurines and wall plaques adapted from Hummel two-dimensional art. I also credit Josephu for the concept of Dubler's producing a non-Hummel line of figurines and wall plaques.

Herbert Dubler, Inc. was in business with that corporate name for only about eight years and was never officially put to rest, corporate-wise, until April 10, 1978, almost thirty-nine years later. The following is a brief review of Certificates of Incorporation, Change of Name, Consolidation, Dissolution, and Amendment that were filed with the State of New York, Department of State.

Herbert Dubler, Inc. was incorporated April 20, 1939, and became Crestwick, Inc., according to Certificate of Change of Name filed December 8, 1947. Alfred E. Wick, who was president of Crestwick, Inc., and who had worked for Herbert Dubler at one time, commented that Crestwick was a name coined by combining the word crest (meaning the highest or best) with his surname, Wick.

Decorative Figurines Corporation was incorporated December 15, 1943, listing the same business address as that of Herbert Dubler, Inc., which was 251 Fourth Avenue, New York 10, New York. One of its directors and stockholders was Alfred E. Wick. When this corporation was dissolved in accordance with Certificate of Dissolution filed September 9, 1953, Joseph Josephu was listed as president.

Artistic Stationery, Inc. was incorporated April 7, 1944, listing the same business address as that of Herbert Dubler, Inc., which was 251 Fourth Avenue, New York 10, New York. One of its directors and stockholders was Alfred E. Wick. Artistic Stationery, Inc., became Sacred Art Publishing Co., Inc. according to Certificate of Change of Name filed November 21, 1949.

Ars Sacra Books, Inc. was incorporated December 5, 1946, and became Crestwick Publishing Corporation, according to Certificate of Change of Name filed January 8, 1948. Sometime between December 5, 1946 and January 8, 1948, Crestwick, Inc., owned by Alfred E. Wick, became sole owner of all outstanding shares of Ars Sacra Books, Inc.

Brochure, page 3. (C. 1942).

Brochure, page 4. (C. 1942).

Certificate of Dissolution of Hummelwerk
Sales, Inc., filed April 10, 1978, page 1.

Hummelwerk Sales Corporation was incorporated June 14, 1957, at which time one of its directors was Franz Goebel of Oeslau bei Coburg, Bavaria, Germany. The records indicate that Hummelwerk Sales Corporation also became Hummel Art, Inc., according to Certificate of Change of Name filed October 18, 1957. But all indications are they both continued as separate entities until their final dissolution in 1978 and 1971, respectively. Hummel Art, Inc. appeared to function in name only as a division within the Hummelwerk Sales Corporation.

Crestwick, Inc. and Hummelwerk Sales Corporation became Crestwick-Hummelwerk Sales, Inc., according to Certificate of Consolidation filed March 30, 1962.

Sacred Art Publishing Company, Inc. was dissolved in accordance with Certificate of Dissolution filed February 9, 1971, by the firm of W. Goebel Porzellanfabrik of Oeslau, West Germany, holder of all outstanding shares of stock in Sacred Art Publishing Company, Inc. Wilhelm Goebel signed the Certificate of Dissolution as president of Sacred Art Publishing Company, Inc. At the time of this dissolution, Wilhem Goebel was known to be a partner in the firm of W. Goebel Porzellanfabrik.

Crestwick-Hummelwerk Sales, Inc. became Hummelwerk Sales, Inc. according to Certificate of Amendment of Certificate of Incorporation filed April 30, 1971.

Crestwick Publishing Corporation was dissolved in accordance with Certificate of Dissolution filed April 29, 1971, by Crestwick-Hummelwerk Sales, Inc., sole stockholder of Crestwick Publishing Corporation.

Hummel Art, Inc. was dissolved in accordance with Certificate of Dissolution also filed April 29, 1971 by Crestwick-Hummelwerk Sales, Inc., sole stockholder of Hummel Art, Inc.

Finally, the corporate demise of Herbert Dubler, Inc. became a reality when, after almost thirty-nine years, Wilhelm Goebel and Kermit Spector, the chairman of the board and the secretary-treasurer, respectively, of Hummelwerk Sales, Inc. did formally sign the Certificate of Dissolution of Hummelwerk Sales, Inc. filed April 10, 1978, of which pages one and two of this several page document are reproduced herein. Note that page one of this final Certificate of Dissolution states,"The name of the corporation is Hummelwerk Sales, Inc. The name under which it was originally incorporated was Herbert Dubler, Inc. . . .''

So with all the incorporations, name changes, consolidations, amendments, dissolutions, and spin-offs, the corporate bloodline that flowed with some semblance of continuity began with Herbert Dubler, Inc., which became Crestwick, Inc., which became Crestwick-Hummelwerk Sales, Inc., which became Hummelwerk Sales, Inc., and was finally put to rest by dissolution on April 10, 1978. Amen.

Final note: Although the corporate entity, Hummelwerk Sales, Inc., was finally dissolved, Hummelwerk lives on at 250 Clearbrook Road, Elmsford, New York, as a division of Goebel Art GmbH, Inc., owned by W. Goebel Porzellanfabrik, West Germany, the only licensed manufacturers of genuine M. I. Hummel figurines.

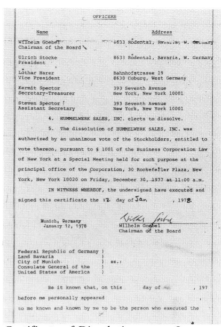

Certificate of Dissolution, page 2.

Copyright Registrations

Even though Herbert Dubler, Inc. was officially incorporated in April 1939, no record of activity in the United States Copyright Office was found until 1942, with copyright entries every year thereafter through 1947, a six-year time frame. Ironically, I have several Dubler notecards in my collection that bear a 1941 copyright date. All copyrights were registered in one of the following classifications:

Class G–works of art.

Class H–reproductions of a work of art.

Class K–prints and pictorial illustrations.

Of the one hundred and seventy copyrights I found registered by Herbert Dubler, Inc. during the above period, the thirty-eight listed herein were registered in Class G or Class H and were credited to talents of either Berta Hummel, Elizabeth Orton Jones, or Joseph Josephu. The balance were registered in Class K as greeting cards and prints and credited to such artists as Charlot Byj, Eva Harta, Eva Harta Heller, Berta Hummel, Mollie Parness, and Beatrice Ryan.

Dubler No. 45 Madonna and Child incised "B. Hummel" very prominently on contoured side of base within a recessed area.

All are incised on the outside edge of base with a copyright symbol, ©, year, and "Herbert Dubler, Inc."

AS-1 foil label, brown on gold, ⅝" h × 1" w. Found only on Dubler Hummel figurines and wall plaques having the "B. Hummel" facsimile signature.

Identifying Dubler Figurines

Figurines and wall plaques listed in the table in this section were produced by Herbert Dubler, Inc. and were executed by Joseph Josephu. In some instances he was also the artist. All items in the Dubler table marked with an asterisk (*) are pictured in this section and most are featured in a family color photograph. The Dubler-assigned names for all are given, accompanied by the Dubler model numbers when known. The name of the artist who created the original artwork (the source for the adaptation) is followed by the copyright number and year. The table lists the model type: figurine or wall plaque. When the model type is unknown, I have indicated my best guess, followed by a question mark (?). This guess is based on considerable research in reviewing the Catalog of Copyright Entries, analyzing the questionable Dubler numbering system, and studying all the figurines and wall plaques in my collection and any others made available to me. With a few noted exceptions, all the Dubler figurines shown are from my personal collection.

None of the Dubler pieces I have seen were marked or incised with a model number or model name. This information was obtained from the Library of Congress Copyright Office Catalog of Copyright Entries and reconfirmed, in part, by a copy of the only known Dubler photo-illustrated brochure, reproduced herein, and by matching the actual figurines with the Dubler names and year of copyright.

You will notice that the lowest known model number is No. 11 for Angel Head and the highest is No. 61 Saint Francis. Did the Dubler numbering system begin with number one and run through sixty-one inclusive, or did it go higher? Not all sixty-one numbers were assigned to a figurine or wall plaque. I did locate two 1945 Copyright Registrations titled Wall Brackets, G-45768 and G-45769, Dubler No. 13 and 14 respectively. These are not included in the table.

I find these Dubler figurines to be inferior only in their plaster-of-paris material content, when compared to the genuine Hummels by Goebel. Joseph Josephu distinguished himself in his original design, detail, and execution of the Dubler line. All appear to be carefully decorated with a coat of high grade enamel paint. The colors used remain strong and vibrant when examined today, forty years later. All were incised on the outside edge of base with a copyright symbol, the year, and "Herbert Dubler, Inc." The bottoms of all the figurine bases were covered with green felt affixed with a foil label of one of the types pictured.

All of the pieces adapted from Berta Hummel's artwork were incised somewhere on the figurine with a signature style "B. Hummel." The "B. Hummel" signature was usually incised on top of base, but not always. Dubler No. 46 Angel's Song was incised "B. Hummel" underside of sheet music held in her hand. Dubler No. 45

Madonna and Child was incised "B. Hummel" very prominently on the side of base in a recessed area. See photograph for detail. In addition, the foil label on the green felt covered base of each figurine read, "Authentic Hummel Figure, Produced by Ars Sacra, Made in U.S.A." The wall plaques were not felt backed, but were affixed with the appropriate foil label.

All the other non-Hummel items carried a foil label that read, "Original Figurine, Designed and Produced by Ars Sacra, Made in U.S.A." There was no affiliation between the "Ars Sacra" (Sacred Art) used by Joseph Müller and the identification "Produced by Ars Sacra," and "The House of Ars Sacra," used for a short period of time by Herbert Dubler, Inc. in their labeling and promotional material.

AS-2 foil label, green on silver, ⅝" h × 1" w. Found only on non-Hummel Dubler figurines and wall plaques.

DF-1 foil label, brown on gold, ⅝" h × ⅞" w. Found only on Dubler and Decorative Figurines Corporation Hummel figurines and wall plaques having the "B. Hummel" facsimile signature.

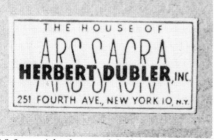

AS-3 varnished paper label, brown on tan, ¾" h × 1½" w. Found on back of framed Dubler prints.

Dubler Figurines, Plaques Photographic Section

Dubler No. 32 Little Bookworm, incised "B. Hummel © 1942 Herbert Dubler, Inc." AS-1 label, 5⅝".

Dubler No. 34 Little Mother, incised "B. Hummel © 1942 Herbert Dubler, Inc." AS-1 label, 4¾". Plain apron.

Dubler No. 32 (back view).

Dubler No. 34 (back view).

Dubler No. 34. Little Mother, incised "B. Hummel © 1942 Herbert Dubler, Inc." AS-1 label, 4¾". Decorated apron.

Dubler No. 35 Little Mailman, incised "B. Hummel © 1942 Herbert Dubler, Inc." AS-1 label, 5⅞".

Dubler No. 34 (back view).

Dubler No. 35 Little Mailman (back view).

Dubler Figurines (continued)

Dubler No. 36 Little Cobbler, incised "B. Hummel © 1942 Herbert Dubler, Inc." AS-1 label, 5⅜".

Dubler No. 37 Doll's Doctor, incised "B. Hummel © 1942 Herbert Dubler, Inc." AS-1 label, 5¾".

Dubler No. 36 (back view).

Dubler No. 37 (back view).

Dubler No. 38 Little Chemist, incised "B. Hummel © 1942 Herbert Dubler, Inc." AS-1 label, 5¾".

Dubler No. 39 Sleepy Baby, incised "B. Hummel © 1942 Herbert Dubler, Inc." DF-1 label, 4½".

Dubler No. 38 (back view).

Dubler No. 39 (back view).

Dubler Figurines (continued)

Dubler No. 40 Mother's Helper, incised "B. Hummel © 1942 Herbert Dubler, Inc." AS-1 label, 5⅝".

Dubler No. 41 Hello! Birdie, incised "B. Hummel © 1942 Herbert Dubler, Inc." AS-1 label, 4". Carol Lucas collection.

Dubler No. 40 (back view).

Dubler No. 41 (back view).

Dubler No. 43 Cactus Puss, incised "B. Hummel © 1942 Herbert Dubler, Inc." AS-1 label, 5⅛". Executed by Joseph Josephu.

Dubler No. 44 Bawling Bennie, incised "B. Hummel © 1942 Herbert Dubler, Inc." AS-1 label, 5½". Executed by Joseph Josephu.

Dubler No. 43 (back view).

Dubler No. 44 (back view).

Dubler Figurines (continued)

Madonna and Child

Madonna and Child, Dubler No. 45, was very possibly an inspired adaptation using the original artwork (1933) "Mary, Queen of May" by Berta Hummel as its basis. The adaptation by Josephu of the "Child" displays much in common, particularly in dress and hairstyle. The "B. Hummel" signature on base of figurine bears a very striking resemblance to the "B. Hummel" signature on the painting. See Identifying Dubler Figurines section for close-up photo of incised signature on base of Dubler Madonna and Child figurine. The painting "Mary, Queen of May" is featured in an article titled "The Other Hummel, The Other Goebel" by Robert Campbell Rowe, publisher of Collector Editions. This painting is shown on page 32, Collector Editions magazine, Spring 1987, Volume 15, Number 1.

Dubler No. 45 Madonna and Child, incised "B. Hummel, Ars Sacra, © 1942 Herbert Dubler, Inc." AS-1 label, 7⅛". Executed by Joseph Josephu.

Dubler No. 45 (back view).

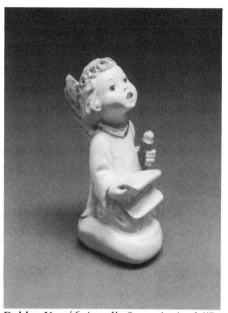

Dubler No. 46 Angel's Song, incised "B. Hummel © 1942 Herbert Dubler, Inc." AS-1 label, 3¾". Executed by Joseph Josephu.

Dubler No. 48 Dentist Dodger, incised "B. Hummel © 1942 Herbert Dubler, Inc." AS-1 label, 4¾". Executed by Joseph Josephu.

Dubler No. 46 (back view).

Dubler No. 48 (back view).

Dubler Figurines (continued)

Dubler unnumbered Boy with Flute, incised "B. Hummel © 1943 Herbert Dubler, Inc." AS-1 label, 5½". Executed by Joseph Josephu.

Dubler unnumbered Band Leader, incised "Ars Sacra © 1943 Herbert Dubler, Inc." AS-2 label, 5¾". Executed by Joseph Josephu.

Boy with Flute (back view).

Band Leader (back view).

Dubler unnumbered Boy with Drum, incised "Ars Sacra © 1943 Herbert Dubler, Inc." AS-2 label, 5½". Executed by Joseph Josephu.

Dubler unnumbered Boy with Saxophone, incised "Ars Sacra © 1943 Herbert Dubler, Inc." AS-2 label, 5⅜" high. Executed by Joseph Josephu.

Boy with Drum (back view).

Boy with Saxophone (back view).

Dubler Figurines (continued)

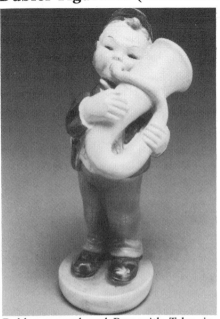

Dubler unnumbered Boy with Tuba, incised "Ars Sacra © 1943 Herbert Dubler, Inc." AS-2 label, 5½". Executed by Joseph Josephu.

Dubler No. 59 Billy Birthday, incised "Ars Sacra © 1945 Herbert Dubler, Inc." 5⅜". Executed by Joseph Josephu.

Boy with Tuba (back view).

Dubler No. 59 (back view).

Joseph Josephu, Sculptor

Joseph Josephu was born January 12 in Vienna, Austria, in the winter of 1889. His family tree traces back to sixteenth century France where Francois Josephi, born in 1577, was titled Baron De Josephi by his good friend Cardinal Richelieu. Josephi being the original family name of Josephu. From his father, a landscape gardener, Josephu learned to love nature and life in all its magnificence. As a young schoolboy in Graz, Austria, Josephu's artistic gifts were revealed at an early age, when he was molding shapes out of whatever material was on hand and carving in wood by the time he was ten years old. Upon counsel from his teachers, he entered the Department of Sculpture of the Municipal Trade School at Graz and studied under Brenneck. At age eighteen Josephu went to Vienna to begin his formal training at the Vienna Academy of Pictorial Arts and concurrently attended the Special School of Sculpture, studying under Professors Bitterlich and Hellmer. While in attendance he won several awards and commendations for his works.

As a lieutenant serving in the infantry during WWI, he was seriously wounded in Italy in 1916. Upon recovering from his wounds, Josephu married in 1918 and completed his studies in 1919. He soon developed his own style, using the human form symbolically in many of his works. Josephu was equally masterful in the mediums of stone, wood, clay, plaster, and in the casting of metal. Theodore Cardinal Innitzer dedicated Josephu's works on two occasions in Vienna, Austria: his sculpture of St. Francis of Assisi that reportedly still stands in Lainzer Vogelschutzpark and a plaque that adorns the Vienna Academy Gymnasium.

When Hitler marched into Austria and imposed conditions Josephu found impossible to accept, his refusal resulted in his being forbidden to work in his homeland. Josephu, his wife, and daughter, sought refuge in this country and settled in New York where he continued to work and create. It was there that the paths of Josephu and the Herbert Dubler Corporation finally crossed in about 1940. I am uncertain whether Josephu was commissioned to do certain works for the Dubler firm on a free-lance basis or directly employed. Regardless of the details of the working relationship, it is obvious that Josephu was very active in the development of the Dubler product line of figurines.

During World War II, Josephu registered several copyrights for Hummel figurines. One particular figurine, Dubler No. 48 Dentist Dodger, with a 1942 copyright registration in the name of Herbert Dubler, Inc., was an adaptation executed by Josephu from the artwork of Berta Hummel. This figurine was showcased in David O. Selznick's 1944 United Artists' $3,000,000 feature movie, *Since You Went Away*, starring Claudette Colbert, Jennifer Jones, Shirley Temple, and Joseph Cotten, among other notable stars. It was a saga of an American family during World War II. In one scene, Joseph Cotten (Lt. Tony Willett) presented Jennifer Jones (Jane) with this Dubler Dentist Dodger figurine (see photograph) as a whimsical memento of her siege with the mumps, which occurred earlier in the movie. At first glance, the ailment of the Dubler figurine could easily be mistaken for mumps instead of a toothache.

Reportedly, Josephu's works can still be found in Europe, South America, Africa, and the United States. Josephu's monument, *Fountain of Refuge*, still stands in the Children's Park of the Pernerstofer-hof in Vienna.

The death of Joseph Josephu, at age 81, occurred on September 13, 1970, but his works live on. His wife, Olga, preceded him in death in 1967. He is survived by his daughter and two grandsons. Syracuse University, New York, maintains a file on Josephu in the George Arents Research Library.

Copy of Joseph Josephu business card. (c. 1940s.) Courtesy of Marc Tantillo, grandson of Joseph Josephu.

Dentist Dodger

Two scenes from David O. Selznick's 1944 United Artist movie classic *Since You Went Away*. Courtesy of Kino International, New York, New York.

Jane (Jennifer Jones) enjoying Dubler figurine presented to her by Lt. Tony Willett (Joseph Cotten).

Dubler No. 48 Dentist Dodger showcased in a cameo role as boy with mumps.

Elizabeth Orton Jones—
Artist/Author/Playwright

Elizabeth Orton Jones in her Highland Park, Illinois, studio. "Elizabeth Orton Jones Papers," University of Oregon Library.

Elizabeth Orton Jones was born June 25, 1910, in Highland Park, Illinois, and became an extremely talented artist, illustrator, and writer of children's books. Her professional work included etchings and paintings, magazine covers, posters, greeting cards, and painted woodenware (children's furniture and toys). Ms. Jones's postgraduate work in painting was pursued in Paris, where she chose to specialize in children as her subject matter. This led to her first published book, *Ragman of Paris* in 1937. Her career summary seems endless, as she has authored and illustrated several children's books and illustrated many more. Ms. Jones later added playwright to her impressive list of accomplishments by writing plays for children. A special collection of her work is being assembled at The Library, University of Oregon, Eugene, Oregon.

From the mid-1930s to the 1940s, Elizabeth Orton Jones admittedly did exceptionally well monetarily, with most of her books being translated into other languages and her painted woodenware selling like proverbial hotcakes. The royalties from her popular greeting cards added to her financial success. During this period, she completed an arrangement with Herbert Dubler, Inc. to publish her greeting cards.

Joseph Josephu used two of her greeting card designs (reproduced herein) for adaptations into figurines for Herbert Dubler, Inc.: Dubler No. 31 Little Skipper, and Dubler No. 33 Tiny Cherub. The Dubler brochure, reproduced in this section, credits E.O. Jones as being the artist of both figurines. My research and discussions with Ms. Jones indicate these were the only two E.O. Jones greeting card designs that were transformed into Dubler figurines.

At this writing, Elizabeth Orton Jones remains active with residence and studio located in Mason, New Hampshire. She is diligently trying to finish some, if not all, the books she herself has started. She looks forward to writing more plays for children and to having those already written published. Hopefully, she will realize the fulfillment of that "inward pointing of the way."

Copy from original greeting card design by Elizabeth Orton Jones used in the adaptation of Dubler No. 31 Little Skipper. "Elizabeth Orton Jones Papers," University of Oregon Library.

Copy from original greeting card design by Elizabeth Orton Jones used in the adaptation of Dubler No. 33 Tiny Cherub. "Elizabeth Orton Jones Papers," University of Oregon Library.

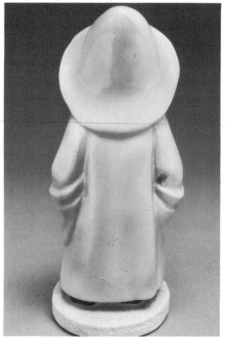

Dubler No. 31 Little Skipper, incised "E. O. Jones © 1942 Herbert Dubler, Inc." AS-2 label, 5⅝".

Dubler No. 31 (back view).

ELIZABETH ORTON JONES

MASON, NEW HAMPSHIRE 03048

October 13, 1985

Larry Wonsch
17720 Common Road
Roseville, Michigan   48066

Dear Larry Wonsch,

I enjoyed talking with you over the phone about days LONG gone
by and difficult to remember in detail.

Thank you for the Polaroid of the figurine of child in yellow
slicker. And then the photocopy of the Cherub which, now that I see
it, I remember, but never would have otherwise. If there were any
other figurines (which I doubt) I would not remember them either,
in all probability.

I have been through files and shelves in my studio but did not
come upon a card of the child in yellow slicker and sou'wester. All
such cards (except for a very few) have been given to the collection
at the University of Oregon Library. I have no originals of the card
designs. Nor any figurines. In speaking with my sister in Evanston,
Illinois, today, I asked if she might have a card of child-in-yellow-
slicker and she thought she might possibly have, in which case she
would send it to me. If so, I would send it to you.

Biographical material pertaining to me is available in WHO'S WHO
in AMERICA, etc., in THE JUNIOR BOOK OF AUTHORS, in a booklet published by University of Oregon Library entitled "The Printer's Life
Is the Life for Me" -- etc., including back numbers of THE HORN
BOOK, publications of the Irvin Kerlan collection, and the like.

I have no old catalogues nor brochures showing the product line
of Dubler or Crestwick. There are no slides of my work available,
to my knowledge.

I am sorry indeed to be such a disappointment to you. However,
as the old folk-tale goes: "What's gone is gone!"

Sincerely yours,

Elizabeth Orton Jones

P.S. I am grateful for your interest.

Correspondence from Elizabeth Orton Jones to author, dated October 13, 1985.

Dubler Wall Plaques

Dubler unnumbered Girl on Apple Tree, wall plaque, incised "B. Hummel © 1943 Herbert Dubler, Inc." AS-1 label 6¼" h × 5" w. Executed by Joseph Josephu.

Dubler unnumbered Boy on Apple Tree, wall plaque, incised "B. Hummel © 1943 Herbert Dubler, Inc." 6¼" h × 5" w. Executed by Joseph Josephu.

(L) Dubler No. (?) Spring Song, Boy, wall plaque. (R) Dubler No. (?) Spring Song, Girl, wall plaque. Both plaques incised "B. Hummel © 1943 Herbert Dubler, Inc." 6¼" h × 5" w. Executed by Joseph Josephu. Marc Tantillo collection. Photograph courtesy Marc Tantillo.

Dubler Figurines, Wall Plaque Value Guide

Key to Symbols: F—figurine. WPLQ—wall plaque. NQV—no quoted value. *Pictured in book.

Dubler Name	Model Number	Artist	Copyright Number	Year	Type	Value
Ali	57	J. Josephu	G-45544	1945	F(?)	$NQV
Angel Head	11	J. Josephu	G-45545	1945	WPLQ(?)	NQV
*Angel's Song	46	B. Hummel	H-2543	1942	F	45
Baba	58	J. Josephu	G-45546	1945	F(?)	NQV
*Band Leader	Unknown	J. Josephu	G-42189	1943	F	95
Band Master	47	B. Hummel	H-2544	1942	F	95
*Bawling Bennie	44	B. Hummel	H-2545	1942	F	95
Betty Bouquet	60	J. Josephu	G-45547	1945	F(?)	NQV
*Billy Birthday	59	J. Josephu	G-45548	1945	F	75
*Boy on Apple Tree	Unknown	B. Hummel	G-42187	1943	WPLQ	37
*Boy with Drum	Unknown	J. Josephu	G-42190	1943	F	95
*Boy with Flute	Unknown	B. Hummel	G-42188	1943	F	95
*Boy with Saxophone	Unknown	J. Josephu	G-42193	1943	F	95
*Boy with Tuba	Unknown	J. Josephu	G-42194	1943	F	95
Bunny	17	J. Josephu	G-45766	1945	WPLQ(?)	NQV
Bunny	18	J. Josephu	G-45766	1945	WPLQ(?)	NQV
*Cactus Puss	43	B. Hummel	H-2546	1942	F	75
*Dentist Dodger	48	B. Hummel	H-2547	1942	F	75
*Doll's Doctor	37	B. Hummel	H-2434	1942	F	95
*Flower Lass	42	B. Hummel	H-2436	1942	F	75
*Girl on Apple Tree	Unknown	B. Hummel	G-42195	1943	WPLQ	37
*Hello! Birdie	41	B. Hummel	G-2437	1942	F	75
*Little Bookworm	32	B. Hummel	H-2438	1942	F	95
Little Bugler	56	J. Josephu	G-45550	1945	F(?)	NQV
*Little Chemist	38	B. Hummel	H-2439	1942	F	95
*Little Cobbler	36	B. Hummel	H-2441	1942	F	95
*Little Mailman	35	B. Hummel	H-2442	1942	F	95
*Little Mother	34	B. Hummel	H-2443	1942	F	85
*Little Skipper	31	E.O. Jones	H-2435	1942	F	120
*Madonna and Child	45	B. Hummel	H-2548	1942	F	350
*Mother's Helper	40	B. Hummel	H-2444	1942	F	95
Sailor Boy	Unknown	J. Josephu	G-42191	1943	F(?)	NQV
Saint Francis	61	J. Josephu	G-45549	1945	F(?)	NQV
*Sleepy Baby	39	B. Hummel	H-2445	1942	F	120
Soldier Boy	Unknown	J. Josephu	G-42192	1943	F(?)	NQV
*Spring Song, Boy	Unknown	B. Hummel	G-42196	1943	WPLQ	37
*Spring Song, Girl	Unknown	B. Hummel	G-42197	1943	WPLQ	37
*Tiny Cherub	33	E.O. Jones	H-2440	1942	F	65

Note: Values are based on POP (plaster-of-paris) Dubler pieces being in very good condition, with only one or two minor paint chips being acceptable. Figurines must have green felt covered bases with the appropriate aluminum foil label affixed.

Metal Dublers

In recent months, several cast-in-metal Dubler figurines, figurine bookends, and figurines mounted in the center of marble or onyx ashtrays have surfaced. In some examples, the base material in which they were cast appears to have been white or pot metal plated in bronze or silver. Others are known to be in cast bronze and/or silver-plated cast bronze. Detail is not as well defined as that of their plaster-of-paris Dubler counterparts. Most pieces were probably cast by making a mold from an original plaster-of-paris Dubler figurine. I credit Joseph Josephu for their genesis.

To my knowledge, all known metal Dublers currently in private collections are included in the Metal Dubler Table. Prior to my discovering the existence of the metal Dublers, I had offered the owner of a Little Mailman figurine ashtray $750, which was half of his asking price. Fortunately for me, he politely declined. Today my offer would be $375, providing the piece was in very good to mint condition and incised "Herbert Dubler, Inc."

Dubler No. 40 Mother's Helper, ashtray, 6¾" high. Marble base. Figurine appears to be silver-plated cast bronze. The 5¾" figurine is incised on edge of base "© 1941. Herbert Dubler, Inc." An exceptionally nice Dubler item. Robert L. Miller Collection.

Dubler No. 40 (back view).

(L) Dubler No. 42 Flower Lass, figurine (POP), incised "B. Hummel, © 1942, Herbert Dubler, Inc." 5½". (R) Dubler No. 42 Flower Lass, figurine/bookend (bronze), 6½" h × 4" w × 4⅜" d. According to owner, the bookend appears to be a bronzeplated white or pot metal with a cast bronze figurine bolted atop the base of bookend. The base of the figurine is incised "B. Hummel, © 1942, Herbert Dubler, Inc." This is one of a pair. Marc Tantillo collection. Photograph courtesy Marc Tantillo.

Dubler No. 48 Dentist Dodger, ashtray, 6½" high. According to Marc Tantillo, the base is either marble or onyx. Figurine appears to be bronze-plated white or pot metal, not cast bronze. Figurine base is incised "B. Hummel, © 1942, Herber Dubler, Inc." Photograph courtesy Marc Tantillo.

Metal Dublers Value Guide

Key to Symbols: F—figurine. F/AT—figurine/ashtray. F/BE—figurine/bookend. WPLQ—wall plaque. NQV—no quoted value. *Pictured in book.

Dubler Name	Model Number	Artist	Type	Value
Little Bookworm (bronze)	32	J. Josephu	F	$125
Little Mailman (bronze)	35	J. Josephu	F	125
Little Mailman (bronze)	35	J. Josephu	F/AT	375
*Mother's Helper (silver)	40	J. Josephu	F/AT	525
*Flower Lass (bronze)	42	J. Josephu	F/BE	350/pr
*Dentist Dodger (bronze)	48	J. Josephu	F/AT	375

Special pricing note: values shown for metal Dublers are for cast bronze and/or cast bronze, silver-plated figurines, whether they be mounted or unmounted. If figurines are cast in white or pot metal, deduct 50 percent from values shown.

Decorative Figurines Corporation

On December 15, 1943, the Decorative Figurines Corporation was formed with its business address listed at 251 Fourth Avenue, New York 10, New York (the same address as that of Herbert Dubler, Inc.). The shareholders of record being Alfred E. Wick, Anna M.A. Glynn, and John P. McArdle. According to the Certificate of Incorporation, the company was formed for the following purposes:

> To design, create, manufacture, purchase, repair, restore, reconstruct, exhibit, sell and generally deal in, as principal or agent, on commission or otherwise, pictures, ornaments, statues, statuettes, figurines, carving, china, pottery, glassware, jewelry, works of art of every class, kind or description, and copies or reproductions thereof; to supply the services of experts in and about the same; to manufacture, buy, sell and deal in art materials and artists' supplies of all kinds.

It appears that this corporation was set up to assist Herbert Dubler, Inc. in producing a portion of their line of Dubler figurines and plaques, and also to produce a separate line of these same items, to be incised "Decorative Figurines Corp.," affixed with their own foil labels that read, "Authentic Hummel Figure, Hand Painted by Decorative Figurines Corp., Made in U.S.A."

Whether or not Joseph Josephu was president of this corporation at its inception is unknown. He signed as president and secretary on the Certificate of Dissolution of the Decorative Figurines Corporation filed September 9, 1953. I did locate a record of brief activity in the United States Copyright Office in Class G for six works of Hummel art registered in 1946. The Catalog of Copyright Entries for that year listed Joseph Josephu as author with the Decorative Figurines Corporation as joint author. The catalog entries noted that four of the figurines were "incised on base: B. Hummel . . .," and the remaining two wall plaques, No. 25 and No. 26, were said to be "from sketch by B. Hummel . . . ." In addition, all six pieces were listed as plaster. These copyright en-

Decorative Figurines unnumbered Country Boy, incised "B. Hummel © 1946 Decorative Figurines Corp." DF-1 label, 4⅞" high. Executed by Joseph Josephu.

Country Boy (back view).

tries indicated the height of the figurines, and, in the case of wall plaques, the height and width were listed. It is obvious by the catalog entries that the sculptor was Joseph Josephu, and the artist whose work he adapted was Berta Hummel. These six Hummel items are listed in the Decorative Figurines Corporation table with current values assigned.

(L) Decorative Figurines No. 26, Hello Darling—Girl, wall plaque. (R) Decorative Figurines No. 25, Hello Darling—Boy, wall plaque. Both incised "B. Hummel © 1946 Decorative Figurines Corp." 6¼" h × 5" w. Executed by Joseph Josephu. Marc Tantillo collection. Photograph courtesy Marc Tantillo.

Decorative Figurines Corporation
Figurines and Wall Plaques Value Guide

Key to symbols: F—figurine. WPLQ—wall plaque. NQV—no quoted value. *pictured in book. Unk—unknown.

Name, Type	Number	Artist	Copyright Number	Year	Size	Value
Brother and Sister F	Unk	B. Hummel	G-2736	1946	5½"	$NQV
Country Boy F	Unk	B. Hummel	G-2734	1946	5"	65
First Shopping F	Unk	B. Hummel	G-2735	1946	5½"	NQV
Hello Darling, Boy* WPLQ	25	B. Hummel	G-2646	1946	6¼" × 5"	38
Hello Darling, Girl* WPLQ	26	B. Hummel	G-2645	1946	6¼" × 5"	38
Spring F	Unk	B. Hummel	G-2733	1946	4¾"	NQV

Note: Values are based on POP (plaster-of-paris) DFC pieces being in very good condition, with only one or two minor paint chips being acceptable. Figurines must have green felt covered bases with the appropriate aluminum foil label affixed.

Beswick Hummel Figurines

Those English Hummel chaps, as I affectionately call them, are an interesting extension of the M. I. Hummel mystique. These fellows roamed about during the same 1940 period as the Dubler kids of New York, but their populace appears smaller. They are like elves in the country-side—out there somewhere, but rarely seen.

Beswick figurines are known to have been produced in eleven different Hummel style models by Beswick of England, now owned by the famous Royal Doulton Company. Unlike the Dublers, Beswick figures appear to be adaptations of Goebel M. I. Hummel figurines rather than original, three-dimensional interpretations inspired by M. I. Hummel art. Nonetheless, these English Hummel copycats are a very unique group. Some Beswicks bear a facsimile M. I. Hummel signature, while others do not. (See photograph of base of Beswick No. 903 Trumpet Boy.) Other Beswicks have been found stamped with "Original Hummel Studios" and "Copyright" in cursive writing style. They are all made from a porcelain-type material and are pleasantly finished in a moderately high gloss. Again, the consensus is that these were produced to take advantage of the Hummel market in the United States that had been lost by Goebel during World War II.

A Beswick value guide is not included here because of their scarcity and extremely variable value in the marketplace. Some prices actually paid for particular Beswick Hummel figurines illustrate this point. To begin with, I paid $12 for Trumpet Boy No. 903 in mint condition at an antique show several months ago. I know of a collector in New York who recently purchased No. 908 Stormy Weather with the M. I. Hummel signature for $45. Another dealer was asking $350 for a heavily crazed, unsigned Beswick Stormy Weather. Farm Boy No. 912 recently sold for $700. These transactions should enable you to appreciate my reluctance to include any type of Beswick value guide.

The eleven Beswick models are:

903	Trumpet Boy	December, 1940
904	Book Worm	December, 1940
905	Goose Girl	December, 1940
906	Strolling Along	January, 1941
908	Stormy Weather	January, 1941
909	Puppy Love	January, 1941
910	Meditation	January, 1941
911	Max and Moritz*	February, 1941
912	Farm Boy	March, 1941
913	Globe Trotter	March, 1941
914	Shepherd's Boy	March, 1941

* This figurine is actually similar to Goebel's Hum. 370 Companions and is listed by Goebel as PFE (Possible Future Edition).

With the exception of Beswick No. 909, Puppy Love, similar to Hum. 1 and Beswick No. 914, Shepherd's Boy, all are pictured in this book.

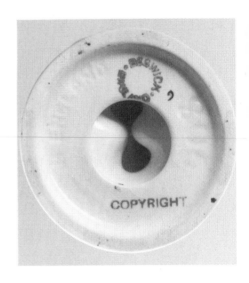

Beswick No. 903 Trumpet Boy, 4⅝". Similar to Goebel's Hum. 97. Circular "Beswick • England" logo and "Copyright" stamped underglaze. Incised "903" and "Made in England."

Beswick No. 903 (back view).

Beswick No. 904 Book Worm, 6⅛". Similar to Goebel's Hum. 3 and Hum. 8. Circular "Beswick • England" logo and "Original Hummel Studios Copyright" in cursive style stamped underglaze. Incised "904." Has two flowers on page. Book pictures in color. Robert L. Miller collection.

Beswick No. 904 (back view).

Beswick Hummel Figurines (continued)

Beswick No. 905 Goose Girl, 6⅛". Similar to Goebel's Hum. 47. Incised "904." No other markings. Note blade of grass between geese. Robert L. Miller collection.

Beswick No. 905 (back view).

Beswick No. 905 (side view). Note blade of grass between geese.

Beswick No. 906 Strolling Along, 4¾". Similar to Goebel's Hum. 5. "Beswick • England" logo and "Original Hummel Studios—Copyright" in cursive style stamped underglaze. Incised "906." Incised side of base with the "M. I. Hummel" facsimile signature. Robert L. Miller collection.

Beswick No. 906 (back view).

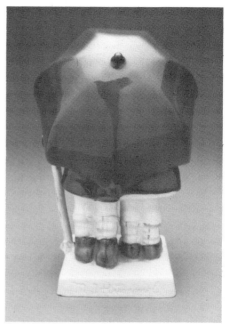

Beswick No. 908 Stormy Weather, 5¾". Similar to Goebel's Hum. 71. Circular "Beswick • England" logo and "Original Hummel Studios Copyright" in cursive style stamped underglaze. Incised "908." Incised back side of base with the "M. I. Hummel" facsimile signature. Robert L. Miller collection.

Beswick No. 908 (back view).

Beswick No. 910 (back view).

Beswick No. 910 Meditation, 5¼". Similar to Goebel's Hum. 13. Circular "Beswick • England" and "Copyright" stamped underglaze. Incised "910" and "Made in England." Robert L. Miller collection.

Beswick Hummel Figurines (continued)

Beswick No. 911 Max and Moritz, 5¾".
Similar to Goebel's Hum. 370, Companions
(possible future edition). Stamped "Copyright" underglaze. Incised "911" and "Made
in England." Robert L. Miller collection.

Beswick No. 911 (back view).

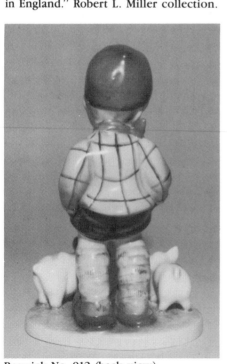

Beswick No. 912 Farm Boy, 6⅛". Similar to
Goebel's Hum. 66. Circular "Beswick •
England" logo and "Copyright" stamped
underglaze. Incised "912" and "Made in
England." Rue Dee Marker collection.

Beswick No. 912 (back view).

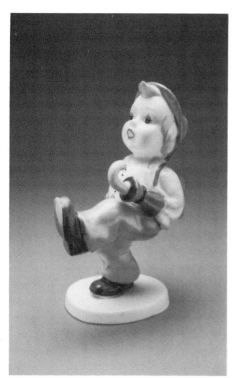 

Beswick No. 913 Globe Trotter, 5″. Similar to Goebel's Hum. 79, except carrying a small satchel in place of basket. Incised "913." Incised back edge of base with the "M. I. Hummel" facsimile signature. No other markings. Robert L. Miller collection.

Beswick No. 913 (back view).

Will the real Hummel Copycats please stand up!

She Loves Me, She Loves Me Not

(L) Goebel's Hum.174, TMK-6. (R) HC-174A. Spain.

Good Friends

(L) Goebel's Hum. 182, TMK-1. (R) HC-182A. Spain.

Spanish Hummel Copycats

If it were not for Rue Dee Marker of Sierra Vista, Arizona, I would never have known of the existence of the Spanish Hummel copycats. Upon hearing that my wife, Millie, and I were planning a trip to Spain, Rue Dee recalled that during his travels there he noticed a couple of Hummel look-alikes, but could not pinpoint exactly where he had seen them.

My search on the Costa del Sol proved fruitless. However, during our stay in Madrid, I had a stroke of luck. While browsing through the stationery department of a large store I was greeted by my first Spanish Hummel copycats: Goose Girl, Umbrella Boy, and Umbrella Girl bookends. Unable to speak Spanish, I had difficulty ascertaining the availability of any others. After returning stateside, I continued my inquiry with the store, El Corte Inglés, with the aid of a translator. After months of persevering, I finally acquired the figurines and bookends shown in this book.

The Spanish creations are true copycats, down to the replication of the very distinctive wooden fence of the Goebel Hummel bookends. The figurines themselves show very good color and detail. The unknown manufacturer created copycats that are in the truest sense a collector's delight.

The hard material composition of the figurines appears to be a cross between a fine grain mortar or grout material and plaster-of-paris. I have coined the name "Popware" as an interim material description until the exact material content is known.

The dozen Spanish Hummel copycats are intermingled throughout the book in black and white photographs and in the Color Section. The figurines are HC-152AA Umbrella Boy; HC-152BA Umbrella Girl; HC-174A She Loves Me, She Loves Me Not; and HC-182A Good Friends. Bookends are BE-60AA Farm Boy; BE-60BA Goose Girl; BE-61AA Playmates; BE-61BA Chick Girl; BE-251AA Good Friends; and BE-251BA She Loves Me, She Loves Me Not. Copycats BE-152AA Umbrella Boy and BE-152BA Umbrella Girl have no Goebel Hummel counterparts as bookends.

Coventry Ware Hummel Copycats

Named by owner Carrie Daum as Dior Studios at the time of its founding in 1932, this Barberton, Ohio, firm was initially formed for the purpose of producing high-quality ceramic artwares and composition plaques. Mrs. Daum renamed the company Coventry Ware, Inc., in 1936 and added plaster-of-paris items to its line in 1940. The exact year production of the Hummel-inspired figurines began is unknown, but it would pre-date 1968, the year the firm reportedly ceased operation.

The detail of the Coventry Ware Hummel children is strongly achieved, despite their lack of color match. All of these desirable copycats are painted in a soft, semi-gloss ivory accented with gold trim. Eyes and eyelashes are executed in black, with faces and lips lightly blushed in red. Bases are cork-covered, with foil D7 or paper D8 labels affixed. Ten Coventry Ware copycats are pictured in the book. See HC-7B Merry Wanderer; HC-8A Book Worm; BE-14AA and BE-14BA Boy and Girl Book Worm bookends; HC-15C Hear Ye, Hear Ye; HC-16D Little Hiker; HC-49F To Market; HC-71-D Stormy Weather; plus BVS-81A School Girl and BVS-82A School Boy bud vases.

Hummel-style Brooches

Long ago, Hummel-inspired metal brooches were made by a company called Creed that designed and manufactured religious jewelry and gifts. Even though they are not jewelry masterpieces, these large, 2½ ″ × 3¼ ″ high, treasures make an interesting addition to any Hummel collection. Those shown are made from white or pot metal and are either silver- or copper-plated. All have a safety clasp pin. Over thirty-five known designs exist that can usually be purchased for ten to twenty-five dollars, depending on their finish, condition, and your "I can't live without it" desire to acquire one.

The brooches appear to be direct adaptations from Sister Hummel's art. Note that many familiar Hummel faces that could very well adopt such names as "Retreat to Safety," "Letter to Santa," "Timid Little Sister," "Little Scholar," and "Little Hiker." I titled six; now you name the other three.

The "Little Scholar" brooch, similar to Hum. 80, featured in the center of the photograph, is made from wood, origin unknown, and valued at two to four dollars.

Hummel-style brooches.

L. E. Smith
Glass Company
Goose Girl Figurine

I first made contact with Henry J. (Hank) Opperman, president of the L. E. Smith Glass Company, in the spring of 1985. I briefed him about my writing a book on Hummel copycat figurines and informed him the book would not be complete unless it included a chapter on the L. E. Smith Glass Company goose girl figurine. His enthusiastic response and continued cooperation in furnishing me with whatever information I might need has enabled me to include this informative chapter.

Accepting an invitation to visit their plant in Mount Pleasant, Pennsylvania, my photographer son, Dan, and I met with Hank Opperman and were allowed to photograph the goose girl molds, plant facilities, and anything else I felt pertinent to the subject. While Dan was busy with cameras and tripods, I unpacked my entire twenty-piece collection of Smith Glass goose girls for detailed evaluation and discussion with Hank as to their individual peculiarities. During this discussion, Hank offered access to their product archives located on the second floor above their administrative offices.

I immediately envisaged shelves upon shelves of glass goose girls, anticipating the discovery of at least a half dozen or so rare prototypes that had been rejected for one reason or another. T'was not to be. For as the three of us proceeded to scour the storage shelves in search of a treasured glass goose girl not already known to me, we found but two common examples — an 8″ green figurine with sculptured base and an 8″ plain base frosted figurine that had been totally painted in white with the goose girl accented in pink. This last piece is now peeling gracefully in my collection. Just when we were ready to end the search, Dan found two very grubby 5¼″ plaster-of-paris goose girls. After much discussion

(L) Author discussing his Goose Girl assemblage with Hank Opperman, president of the L.E. Smith Glass company.

with Hank Opperman and close comparison with the existing glass goose girls in my collection, we concluded that these two figurines must have been the original model inspirations for the molds that produced the many glass goose girls over the years. To my delight, Hank presented me with one of the prototype pair for my personal collection and it is shown in this chapter.

Called Goose Girl, Glass Hummel, Glass Hummel Goose Girl—by whatever appelation used, she is a delightful addition to any true Hummel collector's gatherings. She will dazzle you in amber, amberina, blue, crystal, frosted, green, ruby, iridescent pastel blue and green, two 1980 hand painted frosted editions, plus a 1982 edition in amethyst carnival glass. Produced from time to time by the L. E. Smith Glass Company of Mount Pleasant, Pennsylvania, she is an adaptation possibly inspired by Goebel's Hum. 47 Goose Girl. Born in the late 1930s, in two sizes, she managed to survive not only the Great Depression but the disruptive war years that followed. Finding vintage Goose Girls today is be-

This 5¼″ plaster-of-paris Goose Girl figurine is believed to be the prototype for the L. E. Smith line of 6″ and 8″ glass Goose Girls.

Back view.

coming more difficult, especially in all the colors.

This figurine was produced in a 6″ and an 8″ size (actual heights are 5¾″ and 7¾″, respectively). The 6″ size has more detail than its 8″ counterpart. Both sizes have been found, but not in all colors, with plain and sculptured bases.

The Island Mould Company of Wheeling, West Virginia, made the small 6″ Goose Girl Mold No. 6620 for L. E. Smith Glass Company in 1937. Mold No. 6630 for the 8″ Goose Girl was completed shortly thereafter, whether in the same year or not, no one seems to know. During examination of the cast iron molds, it was pointed out that the mold for the 6″ Goose Girl provided more detail due to its four-part construction as compared to the detail produced by the three-part mold design for the 8″ Goose Girl. Mold No. 6620 used for the 6″ piece has experienced slight production wear, resulting in loss of some definition. This loss, although minute, is easily detected when comparing an early plain base Goose Girl with its sculptured base counterpart.

Some detail variance can also be attributed to glass temperature at the time it was pressed and/or to the glass not being completely pressed into the mold cavity. The resulting variations produced three grades of Goose Girl figurines that mean little to the average consumer but require some guidelines for the discerning collector. Careful examination of the figurines in my collection and others established the following grades of quality, regardless of color.

Grade I—mint condition (no chips, cracks, or grinding repairs). Very good clarity and brilliance (slight seeding acceptable). No detail requirement.
Grade II—mint condition (no chips, cracks, or grinding repairs). Does not meet the Grade I requirements for clarity and brilliance. Shows highly visible, heavy seeding and/or air bubbles in prominent areas.
Premier Grade (produced in 6″ size only)—mint condition (no chips, cracks, or grinding repairs). Very good clarity and brilliance (slight seeding acceptable). This 6″ size must have well defined detail showing (a) hair strands above forehead, (b) eyes,

nose, and mouth, (c) kerchief bow tied back of head, (d) stalks held behind back, (e) sagging stockings.

Note: No "clarity" requirement for Amethyst Carnival.

Smith Glass produced both sizes in only the plain base during the late 1930s and continued production intermittently through 1969. In 1970 the original molds were changed by machining a straw pattern into the figurine's base area inside the mold, producing a sculptured effect in bas-relief on the exterior of the base. This mold change resulted in the demise of the plain base Goose Girl figurine.

The company felt that introduction of the aesthetic sculptured base added sales appeal but, from a collector's viewpoint, this change in base design expanded the number of collectible figurines to thirty-three pieces. Production quantity by color, size, and base design is unknown, as they were unable to locate the old factory production schedules, if, indeed, they still exist. Smith Glass did furnish some production detail on special order pieces.

The Levay Distributing Company of Edwardsville, Illinois, placed a special order with the L. E. Smith Glass Company for the 6″ iridescent pastel blue and 6″ iridescent pastel green glass Goose Girls, Mold No. 6620. Each figurine was to be sequentially numbered beginning with 1/1000, obviously indicating a limited, one-thousand piece edition. This information was hand etched on the underside edge of the oval base with the Levay name followed by the edition number, edition limit, and year 1976. According to the company production records of the Levay Company order, only a combined color total of 542 pieces was ever produced. Therefore, the one-thousand-piece edition in each color was never completed. I was told that this limited edition could very well be completed at some later date, but, after a ten-year production break, I find this extremely doubtful.

Another particular order was for the Amethyst Carnival #6620A produced in 1982. The 1982 production totaled 772 first-quality pieces with no seconds being retained. The Glass Creations Limited brochure advertised this piece in a group of other Amethyst Carnival glassware as

Four-part Mold No. 6620 produces the 6″ Goose Girl figurine.

Three-part Mold No. 6630 produces the 8″ Goose Girl figurine. Note upside-down position of figurines.

Top view. **(L)** Mold No. 6630. **(R)** Mold No. 6620.

199

"Hand Pressed For Glass Creations Limited Only" with a list price of $11.90 each. The Levay Distributing Company also advertised this "6620A 6" Goose Girl" for sale in one of their brochures featuring Amethyst Carnival. I can only assume, since total production of this item by Smith Glass was 772 pieces, that The Levay Distributing Company must have received a portion of this edition.

Hank Opperman seemed receptive to my suggestion regarding marking of future editions of the glass Goose Girl in some special manner to enable collectors to distinguish current and future editions from those produced prior to 1987. I also recommended that the L. E. Smith Glass Company seriously consider producing a 6" edition iridescent golden Goose Girl to commemorate her fiftieth anniversary 1937–1987. Both suggestions are being considered.

The chart of Color Variations, Sizes, Values, and Production Notes illustrates the thirty-three glass Goose Girl models. This chart is based on the assumption that if a piece was produced in an 8" green with plain base, then it was also produced in 6" green with plain base. A crystal 6" sculptured base figurine would have an 8" crystal counterpart. The exception to my assumption, as attested to by Smith Glass company records, are the three 6" iridescent and the two 6" hand-painted frosted figurines. Their records indicate these five Goose Girls were made only in the 6" sculptured base design.

(L) Crystal 6" shown with sculptured base design in bas-relief (straw pattern). Produced 1970 and intermittently thereafter in both sizes. (R) Crystal 6" shown with plain base. Earlier style produced prior to 1970 in both sizes.

Glass Goose Girl, 8" size, resting on one of two iron formers or plungers.

Smith Glass Goose Girl Value Guide

Color Variations, Sizes, Values, Production Notes

Key to symbols: NKP—no known production. L/E—limited edition.
All known color variations are pictured in the Color Section.

Colors	#6620, 6″ Plain Base Pre-1970	#6620, 6″ Sculpted Base 1970 to Present	#6630, 8″ Plain Base Pre-1970	#6630, 8″ Sculpted Base 1970 to Present
Amber	$35	$25	$55	$40
Amberina	40	30	60	45
Blue	45	35	65	50
Crystal	35	25	55	40
Frosted	35	25	55	40
Green	35	25	55	40
Ruby[1]	45	35	65	50

Iridescent Editions

Amethyst Carnival #6620A[2]	NKP	20	NKP	NKP
Pastel Blue[3] L/E	NKP	75 L/E	NKP	NKP
Pastel Green[3] L/E	NKP	75 L/E	NKP	NKP

Hand-Painted Flower Editions

Frosted #6620R[4] (Red roses)	NKP	35	NKP	NKP
Frosted #6620B[4] (Blue forget-me-nots)	NKP	45	NKP	NKP

1. The ruby color Goose Girl was never a planned production color, but an occasional bi-product color created by not being able to totally control the "heat" when producing the amberina figurine. To produce ruby as a production color and maintain a relatively true consistent color balance would require a totally controlled atmosphere.

2. Amethyst Carnival #6620A was produced in 1982. This production totaled 772 first-quality pieces with no seconds being retained. See earlier discussion.

3. The limited edition pieces in pastel blue and green were produced in 1976 exclusively for The Levay Distributing Company (see earlier discussion). This production totaled 484 first-quality pieces and 58 seconds between the two colors. The L. E. Smith Glass Company records did not stipulate exactly how many pieces of each color were produced.

4. The hand-painted flower editions were produced in 1980. The L. E. Smith Glass Company records show total sales of 886 pieces of #6620R (red roses), and 604 pieces of #6620B (blue forget-me-nots).

Except where noted, records of total production by color, size, and year were no longer available. H. J. Opperman, president of Smith Glass, did indicate that a typical production run would be five hundred pieces.

Values are based on Grade I first quality pieces. Deduct 25 percent from values for Grade II second quality pieces. Add 25 percent for Premier Grade pieces produced in 6" size only. See Quality Guide for grading descriptions.

These values were not furnished by the L. E. Smith Glass Company, nor are they representative of the original suggested retail selling prices. Prices are current appraisal values based on personal experience in the marketplace.

(L) The author and (R) president Hank Opperman in his office comparing the peculiarities of two glass Goose Girl figurines. Notice the walled backdrop of original vault lights once produced by the L. E. Smith Glass Company.

Limited Edition 6" iridescent pastel green from Mold No. 6620. Hand-etched "Levay 14/1000 1976" underside of base.

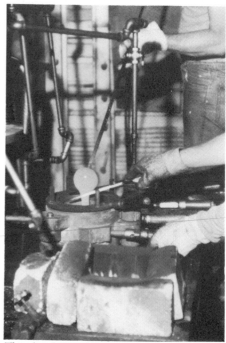

The glass being dropped into the mold, and sheared to proper weight from the gathering iron, will then be pressed into shape.

The Hummel-Hummel Story

Hummel Facts, Volume III by Pat Arbenz, tells another version which he quotes under the column heading, "Saga of 'Hummel-Hummel,' " page 24. If the information Pat quoted is correct, then the story I relate here should begin, "About 140 years ago, . . ."

Rue Dee Marker of Sierra Vista, Arizona, has several interesting variations of this "Hummel-Hummel" figurine in metal and porcelain.

The "Hummel-Hummel" shown is a Goebel product, but is not an "M. I. Hummel" figurine. This 4⅝" piece is incised bottom of base with mold number "LD 58," along with a TMK-6 two-line mark "Goebel W. Germany" underglaze in blue.

Back view.

203

THE HUMMEL-HUMMEL STORY

About 100 years ago, there lived in the German city of Hamburg a man by the name of Hummel. Since Hamburg, like a lot of cities along the German coast did not have good drinking water and very few wells with pure water, Mr. Hummel made a living by catering water to the well-to-do citizens of that town. He was a gruff, gaunt looking character, dressed in a soot-black suit and wearing a stove-pipe hat. With the two wooden buckets hanging from the yoke across his shoulders he was one of the most familiar sights in Hamburg at that time. People, especially children used to taunt him by hollering "Hummel-Hummel" when they passed him, and his short retort always was "Mors, Mors" (kiss my fanny).

Over the years this has become a sort of greeting for Hamburg citizens wherever they meet in the world. It is their good-natured way of saying "hello" and striking up new friendships. The man with the water-buckets and the "Hummel-Hummel" has become the symbol of the city of Hamburg, and the likeness of this man can be found in various shapes and ma-terials in the shops of Hamburg.

Author unknown.

Bibliography

Arbenz, Pat. "Hummel Facts," vol 2., *Plate Collector* June 1976, June 1978.

Arbenz, Pat. "Hummel Facts," vol III. San Marcos, Tex.: Collectors Media, 1985.

Atterbury, Paul, general editor. *The History of Porcelain*. New York: William Morrow and Co., 1982.

Cook Bros. *Wholesale Catalog.* 1984-85, p. 28; 1985-86 pp. 30,31. Chicago.

Derwich, Jenny B. and Dr. Mary Latos. *Dictionary Guide to United States Pottery and Porcelain* (19th and 20th centuries). Franklin, Mich.: Jenstan Research, 1984.

Ehrmann, Eric. *Hummel: The Complete Collector's Guide and Illustrated Reference,* 1st ed., 2nd printing. Huntington, NY: Portfolio Press, 1976.

Florence, Gene. *The Collector's Encyclopedia of Occupied Japan Collectibles.* Paducah, Ky.: Collector Books, 1976.

Florence, Gene. *The Collector's Encyclopedia of Occupied Japan Collectibles,* Second Series, 1979; Third Series, 1987. Paducah, Ky.: Collector Books.

Gee, Robert W. "Occupied Japan Collectors Club Newsletter," vol 1, no. 8. August 1982; vol 1, no. 9. November 1982. Torrance, Ca.

"Glass Creations Limited." Brochure. Fairfax, VA.

Goebel. "Guide for Collectors • *Katalog für Sammler.*" Rödental, West Germany: W. Goebel Porzellanfabrik, 1983.

Goebel. "M.I. Hummel—Figurines Guide for Collectors." English/German catalog. Rödental, West Germany: W. Goebel Porzellanfabrik. n.d.

Horn, Susan Farish. "Ceramics Glossary: Review." *Antique Monthly,* September 1984.

Hotchkiss, John F. *Hotchkiss' Handbook to Hummel Art: With Current Prices.* Des Moines, Ia.: Wallace-Homestead Book Co., 1982.

Hotchkiss, John F. *Hummel Art.* Des Moines, Ia.: Wallace-Homestead Book Co., 1978.

Hotchkiss, John F. *Hummel Art II.* Des Moines, Ia.: Wallace-Homestead Book Co., 1981.

"House of Ars Sacra, The." Herbert Dubler, Inc. Brochure. n.d.

Klamkin, Marian. *Made in Occupied Japan: A Collector's Guide.* New York: Crown Publishing, 1976.

Luckey, Carl F. *Hummel Figurines and Plates,* 6th ed. Florence, Ala.: Books Americana, 1985.

Miles Kimball of Oshkosh. Fall & Winter Catalog, 1946-47 ed. Oshkosh, Wis.

Miller, Robert L. *Hummel Authorized Supplement to 1st Edition of Hummel: The Complete Collector's Guide and Illustrated Reference.* Huntington, New York: Portfolio Press, 1979.

Miller, Robert L. *The No. 1 Price Guide to M. I. Hummel,* 2nd ed. Huntington, New York: Portfolio Press, 1983.

Miller, Robert L. and Eric W. Ehrmann, *M. I. Hummel: The Golden Anniversary Album.* Huntington, New York: Portfolio Press, 1984.

Rowe, Robert Campbell. "The Other Hummel, the Other Goebel." *Collectors Editions,* vol 15, No. 1. Spring 1987.

Schmid Bros. *Formation of an Artist: The Early Works of Berta Hummel.* Randolph, Mass.: Schmid Bros., 1980.

Selznick, David O. *Since You Went Away.* United Artist Production 1944. Movie.

Shumpert, Gwen. "Gwen's Glassline." *Glass Review,* April 1980.

Smith Glass Co., L. E. Factory Outlet Plant Tour brochure.

Spence, Sandra. *Origin and Growth of the L. E. Smith Glass Company.* Mount Pleasant, Pa.: 1956.

Tantillo, Marc, information on Joseph Josephu.

The Hummel, Drawings by Berta Hummel with Light Verse. Munich, West Germany: Verlag Ars Sacra, Joseph Müller, 1972.

United China & Glass Co. Gift catalog. 1985, p. 84; 1986, p. 150. New Orleans, La.

United States Library of Congress, Copyright Office, Catalog of Copyright Entries: Part 4. New Series: 1942 vol 37, no. 8; 1943 vol 38, no. 1; 1944 vol 39, no. 1; 1945 vol 40, no. 1; 1946 vol 41.

United States Library of Congress, Copyright Office, Catalog of Copyright Entries: Third Series, vol 1, parts 7-11A, no. 1.

University of Oregon Library. *Imprint: Oregon.* "Printer's Life Is the Life for Me." E. O. Jones. vol 1, no. 1. Spring 1974.

Wiegand, Sister M. Gonsalva, OSF. *Sketch Me, Berta Hummel!* Eaton, Ohio: Robert L. Miller, Miller Enterprises, 1978.

Willitt's Designs Catalog. 1985, p. 47. Petaluma, Ca.

Index

Key to Symbols: **BE**—bookend. **BVS**—bud vase. **CDL**—candleholder. **DFC**—Decorative Figurines Corporation. **F**—figurine. **F/AT**—figurine/ashtray. **F/BE**—figurine bookend. **HC**—Hummel copycat figurine. **HCM**—Hummel mini copycat. **MBX**—music box. **MC**—Mel copycat. **PLQ**—plaque. **PLQF**—plaque figurine. **PTR**—planter. **REL**—religious message figurine. **RMF**—revolving musical figurine. **SPS**—salt and pepper shaker. **TLP**—table lamp. **TPK**—toothpick holder. **WPLQ**—wall plaque. **WVS**—wall vase. Photographs of subject indicated by boldface type.

211

About the Author

L awrence L. Wonsch is a collector's collector with an aptitude for the gathering of objects for personal satisfaction without regard for their historical significance. A collector of match covers in his teens, then over the years: edged weapons, Japanese gunpowder flasks, arms and armor of feudal Japan, Ispanky figurines, canoes and canoe paddles (scale model, toy, novelty, souvenir), M. I. Hummel figurines, and currently, but not finally, Hummel copycats. Tomorrow—who knows? He is past member of many and a current member of only those collector organizations related to his present collecting interests.

Professionally, Mr. Wonsch is Corporate Treasurer and Manager of Purchasing for Standard Machine and Tool Company, a leading special machine tool builder based in Roseville, Michigan. He is a Certified Purchasing Manager (C.P.M.) and has been a member of both The Purchasing Management Association of Detroit and the National Association of Purchasing Management since 1962. Born, raised and educated in Michigan, he currently resides in Roseville with his wife, Millie.

About the Photographer

A fter experiencing a variety of hobby phases during his teen years, Dan Wonsch always returned to photography as his main interest. A life-long resident of Michigan, Dan graduated from Brablec High School, Roseville, in June, 1978. While working in the machinist trade during the day, he successfully completed photography courses at night at Macomb Community College, Warren, Michigan. Making his career decision, Dan enrolled at the prestigious Center For Creative Studies, College of Art and Design, Detroit, Michigan, as a full-time student in September 1983, majoring in Photography. Upon earning his Bachelor of Fine Arts degree in May, 1987, Dan will continue his present free-lance business, while establishing himself professionally in the very competitive field of photography.